THE WAY OF THE CREATIVE FOOL

How to Bust Through Your Blocks and
Unleash Your Full Creative Potential…
in 12½ Super-Simple Steps!

Mark David Gerson

THE WAY OF THE CREATIVE FOOL
How to Bust Through Your Blocks and Unleash Your Full Creative Potential…in 12½ Super-Simple Steps!

Copyright © 2026 Mark David Gerson
All rights reserved

No part of this book may be reproduced, stored in a retrieval system or transmitted by any means, electronic, mechanical, photocopying, recording or otherwise, without written permission from the author, except for the inclusion of brief quotations in critical reviews and certain other noncommercial uses permitted by copyright law. And no part of this book may be used or reproduced in any manner for the purpose of training artificial intelligence technologies or systems.

Published by MDG Media International
18291 N. Pima Rd., Suite 110-177
Scottsdale, AZ 85255

www.mdgmediainternational.com

Library of Congress Control Number: 2025949907

ISBN: 978-1-950189-37-3 (print)
ISBN: 978-1-950189-38-0 (ebook)

Author Photograph: "A Dog and His Fool"
*A selfie captured halfway through
the Yellow Brick Road journey mentioned in Step #5*

More About Mark David Gerson
www.markdavidgerson.com

The Mark David Gerson School of Writing
www.gersonwritingschool.com

Praise for The Fool

The Way of the Fool
The Way of the Imperfect Fool
The Way of the Abundant Fool
The Way of the Creative Fool

It will transform your life! Don't just read it. Live it!
Rev. Brendalyn Batchelor – Unity Santa Fe

Making any life-changing decision takes courage and support. This book has afforded me both.
Isa de Quesada – Tillamook, OR

Simple but powerful!
Dave Kerpen – author of "The Art of People"

Inspired and inspiring… A powerful but accessible guide.
Dan Stone – author of "Ice on Fire"

A must-read guidebook to living your richest, most authentic life!
Joan Cerio – author of "Hardwired to Heaven"

Mark David Gerson is a master…one of the great teachers!
Rev. Mary Omwake – Unity of Maui

A transformational must-read!
Laura Dorfman – Salamanca, NY

Lays the groundwork for you to step out of your own way and pursue your dreams… A book that frees you from everything holding you back!
Ted Wiga – San Francisco, CA

More from Mark David Gerson

Self-Help & Personal Growth

The Book of Messages: Writings Inspired by Melchizedek

Memoir

Acts of Surrender: A Writer's Memoir
Dialogues with the Divine: Encounters with My Wisest Self
Pilgrimage: A Fool's Journey
All That Matters Is That I'm Writing
Hello, Yellow Brick Road: The Fool's Journey Continues
A Lifetime of Miracles: A Memoir of Magic and Manifestation

Fiction

The MoonQuest • The StarQuest • The SunQuest
The Bard of Bryn Doon • The Lost Horse of Bryn Doon
The Sorcerer of Bryn Doon

Sara's Year • After Sara's Year • The Emmeline Papers

For Writers & Aspiring Writers

The Voice of the Muse: Answering the Call to Write
The Voice of the Muse Companion: Guided Meditations for Writers
From Memory to Memoir: Writing the Stories of Your Life
Organic Screenwriting: Writing for Film, Naturally
Birthing Your Book…Even If You Don't Know What It's About
The Heartful Art of Revision: An Intuitive Guide to Editing
Writer's Block Unblocked: Seven Surefire Ways to Free Up Your Writing and Creative Flow
Time to Write • Write with Ease • Write in the Flow!
Free Your Characters, Free Your Story
Write to Heal • Journal from the Heart

*If I could tell you what it meant,
there would be no point in dancing it.*

ISADORA DUNCAN

*There are no rules of architecture
for a castle in the clouds.*

G.K. CHESTERTON

To the Creative Fool in us all

Contents

Introduction	9
Getting Started	13
Your Muse and You	19
The Steps	29
Step #1. Break Old Rules to Break New Ground	33
Step #2. Fire Up Your Passion	55
Step #3. Be Daring!	71
Step #4. Be Authentic	89
Step #5. Dive into the Mystery	109
Step #6. Create in the Moment	125
Step #7. Trust Your Muse	141
Step #8. Free Your Creation	161
Step #9. Strive for Excellence, Not Perfection	179
Step #10. Commit to Your Passion	195
Step #11. Reject Rejection	213
Step #12. Celebrate Your Creations...and Your Creativity	237
Step #12½. Embrace Your Vision	253
Beyond the 12½th Step	269
A Community of Creative Fools	275
The Way of the Creative Fool and You	279
Afterword: The Creative Fool and I	281
Appreciation	285
About the Author	289

Introduction

I NEVER WANTED to be a writer, or any kind of storyteller. And I definitely haven't been at it as long as all those authors who've known since they were little that they wanted to write books. Me? I hated writing...mostly because I was certain I wasn't creative.

That wasn't true only of writing. I hated art class nearly as much as I hated English class (although I loved to read). As for music (I played the alto sax in high school), I managed only because I could follow the notes and other notations and never had to improvise.

In school, I gravitated toward math and science and, later, business...anything where, if I obeyed the rules, I was guaranteed a right answer. Through it all, I kept as far as possible from anything involving self-expression. All creativity's shades of gray terrified me.

The sole exception was photography.

From the moment I got my first cameras — a Brownie, then an Instamatic — I loved capturing the world around me on film. Still, that wasn't creative, not to my mind. All I was doing was peering through a viewfinder and pressing a shutter, the visual equivalent of hitting the record button on the portable reel-to-reel Sony I got for my bar mitzvah.

Even once I became a writer (a story I tell in Step #2), I wasn't a *creative* writer. "I'm a gifted wordsmith," I would grudgingly concede when referring to the press releases, news stories, magazine features and institutional handbooks I penned into my late thirties as a staff and, later, freelance writer. But creative? No way.

I have often wondered what blocked me all those decades ago…and for so many years after. What stopped me from seeing myself as creative? Was there some inciting incident in my childhood that shut me down? Did one of my parents say or do something that blinded me to my gifts? Was it my older sister? A neighbor? A schoolyard bully? One of my teachers?

In my writing workshops, participants often introduce themselves by saying, "I used to love to write until—" That "until" is nearly always a high school teacher or college professor.

Me? I don't remember *ever* loving to write…or sing… or draw.

What could have happened?

It doesn't matter. What matters is that whatever it was, whoever it was, I finally found my way through and past it, past them. My way was the Way of the Fool, the Way of the *Creative* Fool…not that I could have characterized it that way at the time.

What is the Fool? And what does it have to do with creativity?

The Fool is more than the first card of a tarot deck or the joker in a standard deck. It's more than a game piece or metaphysical divination device. It's an archetype, a sort of mythic character that lives inside us — inside the collective unconscious of all humanity. Like all archetypes, it speaks to our very essence as human beings…to an aspect of our consciousness that not only evokes powerful emotions and reveals who we are at our deepest levels, but that can offer powerful tools for living that are available to all of us.

The archetype of the Fool offers a particularly potent set of tools to help us access, acknowledge, embrace and express our innate creativity and to do it authentically, fearlessly and unselfconsciously. Moreover, the relevance of those tools is not limited to a single form of creative expression. Music, writing, photography, filmmaking, painting, drawing, sculpture: The wisdom of the Fool applies to all forms and all media. All genres too.

It doesn't have to be a traditional type of creative expression. Crafting, carpentry, gardening, the culinary arts, software development, any form of invention or design: The wisdom of the Fool applies to those as well.

Nor does it matter where you are with a specific project or where you find yourself on your creative journey. Perhaps you're unsure how or where to start, or are looking for a way to go deeper or shift focus. Or perhaps, as I was, you're feeling blocked in your creativity or are in denial that you *are* creative. (Hint: You are.) Here, too, the wisdom of the Fool has the answers you need, whether you're a beginner or a longtime creator, whatever you are creating or are feeling called to create.

What *The Way of the Creative Fool* does is take all that wisdom and simplify it into an easy-to-follow roadmap guaranteed to propel you forward on your creative journey.

How? By helping you…

- Break out of the straitjacket of everyone else's rules, methods and techniques.
- Ditch your preconceptions and others' expectations.
- Take the risks and leaps of faith that fuel originality.
- Abandon perfectionism and control.
- Trust your voice and vision.
- Commit to your passion and put that commitment into practice.

- Transcend others' judgments…and your own.
- Celebrate your creations and your creatorship.

The 12½ steps of *The Way of the Creative Fool* are designed to do all that and more — clearly and effectively. Better still, none of the steps is difficult to implement. Of course not. Why would the Fool choose to walk a complex, complicated path?

At the same time, *The Way of the Creative Fool* is unlikely to be entirely alien to you. There's a good chance you will recognize at least a few of its 12½ steps. The fact is, none is radical or new. How can they be when they're built on a timeless archetype that already lives as a potential within each of us?

Here's what *is* revolutionary and groundbreaking: distilling the age-old wisdom of the Fool into a clear, step-by-step guide — a guide to freeing your creative spirit, unleashing your creative potential and expressing your creative passion…more naturally, effortlessly and spontaneously than you ever imagined possible.

The next chapter will offer you some tips and best practices for using *The Way of the Creative Fool*. It will also answer the most burning question you may have had when you first saw this book's subtitle: "Why 12½ steps? Why not thirteen?"

So what are you waiting for? Turn the page and join me for a journey into the heart of *your* creativity…on the Way of the Creative Fool!

Getting Started

How to Use This Book

IF YOU HAVE WORKED with any other books in my *Way of the Fool* series, you might be tempted to skip this chapter. Yet even though many of its suggestions are similar to those in those other books, I encourage you to glance at these, if only as a quick refresher.

Of course, if this is your first Fool-ish book, take a few moments to Fool-ly read what follows.

First, the format of *The Way of the Creative Fool*: Each of the book's 12½ steps consists of several elements...

- stories — mine and others' — that demonstrate the step in action

- stories that link the step to the Fool archetype

- inspiration, exercises, tips and meditations to help you experience the step and integrate it into your creative life

- a simple affirmation-like declaration to anchor that step into your creative life

Is there an ideal way to use these elements? Of course not. That would hardly be true to the way of the Fool. Even had I the audacity to do so, Step #1 urges you to "break old rules to break new ground." So what would be the point?

As Step #1 also points out, "there is no single right way or wrong way. ... The only right way is your way." So find the way through this book that works best for you. Specifically…

- Don't feel compelled to work with the 12½ steps in the order presented here. Should you sense a sequence that better serves your needs, go for it.
- Don't consider yourself to have failed should you skip any exercises, explorations or meditations. At the same time, be aware of your reasons for doing so.
- Always trust your Muse (Step #7), and do your best to not let your inner critic take charge of the process or rule your decisions (Step #11). If you choose to pass over an exercise for any reason, consider returning to it at a later date.
- Feel free to amend any exercises or declarations to better fit the specifics of your form, medium, genre and current situation.
- Use your discernment to stay with each step until you feel a subtle or not so subtle shift in consciousness and awareness. If issues surface for you, while working with *The Way of the Creative Fool* or after you have completed it, repeat any step or exercise that feels relevant.
- As for the declarations, they are designed to be used daily or as often as you feel the need.

Your Way of the Fool Journal

Start a Way of the Fool journal as a companion to your work with this book. Use it, of course, for the exercises and explorations included with each of the 12½ steps. Use it as well for any other Fool-related experiences you choose to probe or chronicle. If you're visually/design oriented, consider using a notebook with unlined pages to free you to sketch or draw, should that feel like your best response to any exercise.

Your Way of the Fool journal can be a dedicated journal or you can integrate it into an existing journal. If you worked with any other books in this series, keep going with the journal you started for that book.

Your journal can be a physical notebook or it can be a journal you keep on your computer, tablet or smartphone, either using your device's writing or drawing software or a dedicated journaling app. If you're more comfortable filming or recording your thoughts and impressions, store the resulting files in a "Creative Fool" folder for easier access. Or create a multimedia journal that incorporates all of those.

Regardless, have your Way of the Fool journal handy whenever you work with the book.

Guided Meditations

The Way of the Creative Fool includes a series of guided meditations, guided visualizations and meditative journeys to help you work with many of the book's 12½ steps.

How to Use a Meditation

- Record it yourself for playback (record it into your phone's voice memos app for easy access).
- Have a friend or creativity partner read the meditation to you, then return the favor.
- Read the meditation slowly and receptively, following its directions and suggestions.

Should you prefer a professionally guided approach, I have recorded versions of five of this book's meditations on *The Voice of the Muse Companion: Guided Meditations for Writers*:

- "Meet Your Muse"
- "Create from the Heart" ("Write from the Heart" on the recording)
- "The Butterfly"
- "Let Judgment Go"
- "Taming Your Inner Critic"

Stream any of these for free as a subscriber to Apple Music, YouTube Music or Amazon Music Unlimited. If you don't subscribe to one of those services, purchase the individual tracks from Amazon or Apple Music.

Alternatively, download the complete *Voice of the Muse Companion* album from my website[1], Apple Music, Amazon or CD Baby.

(Note that *The Voice of the Muse Companion* is geared toward writers, so individual meditations may differ in some ways from the versions scripted in the book.)

However you proceed, find a quiet, private place where you can sit or lie down comfortably and where you won't be disturbed or distracted, either during the meditation or while you're journaling afterward. Be sure to turn off your phone or set it to Do Not Disturb or Airplane mode, and silence any other electronic devices.

A Few Notes About Language

The Fool knows no gender. Unfortunately, the English

---

[1] www.markdavidgerson.com/musemeditations

language wasn't designed for that kind of imprecision. To compensate, *The Way of the Creative Fool* generally alternates between "she" and "he" when referring to the Fool.

Throughout *The Way of the Creative Fool*, I use inclusive words and phrases like "creator," "creative artist," "creative project" and "creative expression." As you move through the book, feel free to replace those general terms with words and phrases directly related to you and to your form, medium and genre.

Why 12½ Steps?

I promised an answer, and here it is…sort of.

I could have presented you with thirteen steps instead of 12½. Or fourteen, given that the chapter titled "Beyond the 12½th Step" is itself a sort of step. Yet doesn't 12½ sound, well, more Fool-ish? And being Fool-ishly creative (and creatively Fool-ish) is what this book is all about. So let's get past "Getting Started" and *get started*.

Your Muse and You

What's a Muse?

IN GREEK MYTHOLOGY, the nine Muses were the daughters of gods Zeus and Mnemosyne. Goddesses in their own right, each Muse presided over an aspect of the arts and sciences — from history to hymns, comedy to poetry, astronomy to tragedy.

Today, however personified, the Muse has come to symbolize creative inspiration, not solely for traditional artists but for all of us. Or, as I put it in the "Meet Your Muse" meditation later in this section, your Muse is "the being that...embodies your purest creative source, that font of creative energy, inspiration and revelation that we all have within us."

By the way, it doesn't matter whether you're creating on an easel or in the kitchen, on a notepad or in the garden, you *are* a creative artist. Don't let anyone tell you otherwise. And whether you're conscious of it or not, you probably have a Muse.

For too many creative artists, the Muse is a capricious adversary that makes itself available somewhat reluctantly and merely when conditions are perfect. "My Muse has deserted me," they grouse. Or, "My Muse refuses to cooperate." Or, "My Muse is shy."

Those artists have it all wrong. Muses are never shy. It's we artists who are deaf or, rather, choose not to listen. Muses are never uncooperative. We're the ones who refuse to cooperate. Muses never desert, hold back or resist. We desert, hold back and resist all the time.

What kind of relationship do you have with your Muse? Do you have any relationship with your Muse? If you don't, you soon will…starting with the "Meet Your Muse" guided meditation coming up in a few pages.

What's a "Muse Stream"?

The Muse Stream is a concept I originally developed to help promote creative flow for writers, but its core philosophy works in all creative disciplines. I'll talk more about how you can use it to free up any creative expression in Step #1.

Basically, though, creating on the Muse Stream means creating without stopping — without stopping to think, alter or correct. It means creating without second-guessing, without censoring. It means creating without worrying about how others might judge you.

This simple technique prevents your head from getting in the way of your heart and stops your personality mind from blocking the free flow of your most authentic, most creative expression — however and wherever you feel called to express yourself.

For now, let's focus on how you can use the Muse Stream in your Way of the Fool journal and for some of the exercises in *The Way of the Creative Fool*.

If you're familiar with terms like "free writing," "automatic writing," "stream of consciousness writing" or "morning pages," you already have a sense of what writing on the Muse Stream is about: a wholesale, uncensored, right-brain outpouring onto the page that can get you past your inner critic, inner censor, analytical mind and second thoughts to that place where your most truthful feelings and reflections reside.

The key, as I noted above, is to write without stopping... without stopping to edit, without stopping to stress about spelling, punctuation or grammar, without looking back over what you have already written, without letting self-judgment dam up your flow. It's about moving forward.

That's the ideal. On the Way of the Creative Fool, however, life does not always play out as expected. So what happens when the words won't come? What happens when you feel stuck? What happens when fear or anxiety aborts the flow of your freest expression?

Here are a couple of tips to use in your journaling or for any kind of Muse Stream writing:

- *Repeat.* Repeat anything to keep your pen or fingers in motion: the previous word or sentence, your opening word or sentence, or anything at all, even if it's "I don't know what to write" or "This is dumb."

- *Free-associate.* Let one word trigger the next — whatever leaps to mind, however silly. Let that word trigger the next and the next and so on...until the flow returns.

- *Get Whimsical.* Make up words...words that sound funny...words that sound weird...words that don't exist in any known dictionary. Make one up, jot it down...then another...then another...then another. This playful act tricks your inner censor into dropping its guard. Soon, nonsense words will become Muse-sense words and your flow will resume. Alternatively, repeat something mindless like la-la-la.

- *Get More Whimsical.* If you're writing longhand, turn your page sideways or upside down. Or start writing in a spiral or around the edges of the page. Or exchange your conventional black or blue ballpoint or roller ball for a brightly colored pen, pencil or marker or for a crayon, pastel or paintbrush. Such startling changes work to stun your censorious mind and free up your flow.

- *Switch Languages.* If you're fluent enough in another language, or if English isn't your first language and you're struggling for an English term, switch languages for a while.

- *Write Your Breath.* The best way to remain present and in the flow is through your breath. Write, "I am breathing in" as you inhale and "I am breathing out" as you exhale. Keep repeating the pair of sentences and keep matching your breath with what you're writing until your flow returns. And it will. Your breath may also help you retrieve words, ideas and images from the deepest wells of your unconscious mind, which is the realm of the Fool.

- *Write Blind.* Close your eyes, breathe deeply and write without watching your hand, screen, keyboard or notepad. Removing your attention from the external act of writing and placing it on your breath will carry you inward, away from the source of your anxiety and toward the source of your words. Remember to breathe, to turn your page if you're writing longhand and, if you're using a physical keyboard, to keep feeling for the notches on the F and J keys. *Caveat*: Proceed with caution. It's easy when writing longhand to write over what you have already written, and when on a computer or mobile device to hit the wrong keys. I've done both. I once hand-wrote a half-dozen pages on top of each other because I was so in the flow that I forgot to turn the page. There was also one writing session where I typed several pages in a (fortunately decipherable) "code," when one hand strayed a single key to the right.

- *Doodle.* If all else fails and you're writing longhand or on a compatible tablet, draw or doodle. Frankly, it doesn't matter what you do, as long as you keep *something* flowing onto your page or screen. Before long, squiggles will make way for words, words will form into sentences and you will forget that you ever felt stuck.

Bottom line: Do *anything* to keep words flowing onto your page.

What Are Keywords and Key Phrases?

In our everyday lives, keys unlock that which has been locked and give us access to that which has been hidden away. A keyword or key phrase does something similar. When we launch a Muse Stream journaling session, or any kind of writing session, from a keyword or key phrase, that "key" can admit us into inner realms that may have been veiled from our conscious awareness. It can even reawaken memories long ago forgotten. That's what makes keywords and key phrases such powerful journaling tools when used with the Muse Stream.

In several exercises in *The Way of the Creative Fool*, I start you off with a keyword or key phrase. Just so you know, it doesn't matter whether your journaling strays from the surface theme or topic of a keyword or key phrase. What matters is that you let the Muse Stream carry you where it will, without censorship or judgment, freeing it to gift you with a deeper understanding of some aspect of yourself, your creativity and your life.

Meditation: Meet Your Muse

Have your Way of the Fool journal handy to record your thoughts, feelings and impressions. Allow at least 30 minutes for this experience, longer if you plan further explorations in your journal once you have completed the meditation.

My studio recording of "Meet Your Muse," one nearly identical to this version, is available for download or streaming[1] as part of "The Voice of the Muse Companion: Guided Meditations for Writers."

Revisit "Getting Started" to find out how to access the recording, as well as for tips on how best to use all this book's meditations, visualizations and meditative journeys.

Relax. Close your eyes. Get into a comfortable position. Let your shoulders drop. And drop some more.

Take a few deep breaths, breathing in calm and quiet, breathing out fears, fatigue, stress.

You're relaxed but alert. Awake and aware. Moving into a quiet place. A deep place. A place of creative freedom, creative vision, creative awakening.

In your mind's eye, see a door. A beautifully crafted door. Handcrafted. A work of art.

Perhaps it's a new door, newly discovered. Perhaps it's ancient, as old as time, just waiting for you to rediscover it. See it or sense it…however you see it or sense it.

This is your doorway of inner creative vision. Walk up to it. Run your hand over it. Feel its texture…its richness… its depth.

As you touch the door, it swings open. The door to

---
[1] Search the relevant site/store for "Mark David Gerson meet your muse."

your inner creative vision will always swing open at your touch…if you let it.

You are the key.

Now the door swings open and you step across the threshold. Into a wondrous place. Perhaps you recognize this place. Perhaps it's new.

Whatever you see or sense and however you see or sense it is perfect, perfect for you, in this moment.

See or sense this place, this wondrous place. See or sense it fully, using all your senses.

What does it look like? What colors do you see? How is the light? Do you hear any sounds? Smell any smells?

Reach out and touch something. Feel its texture.

What is the spirit of this place? What does it feel like, to you?

Now, coming toward you through this wondrous place, coming toward you bathed in light, is your Muse. Your creative spirit. The being, spirit or essence that embodies your purest creative source, that font of creative energy, inspiration and revelation we all have within us.

This is yours. Unique to you.

However it manifests, whatever you see, sense or feel of it, is right for you. In this moment.

Open your mind and heart. Allow she, he or it to come to you in whatever form it comes, recognizing that its form can change from moment to moment, mood to mood, creative project to creative project.

There is no right or wrong image, right or wrong way. There is only the way you see or sense, and what you see and sense. And it's perfect. For you.

What does your Muse look like? Feel like to you?

See or sense it fully. Again, use all your physical senses — sight, touch, smell, taste, sound. And your intuitive senses — feeling, spirit, essence.

Your Muse now stands before you, and you greet each other in whatever way feels right, taking all the time you need.

Now, you and your Muse begin a special dialogue.

Perhaps your Muse has a message for you. Perhaps you have questions for your Muse — questions about a project, questions about which is the right project for you right now, or general questions about your creative journey, your creative purpose, your creative life.

Be open to whatever comes up. Let the dialogue go where it will.

Take thirty seconds of silence for this conversation. Open your eyes to record it in your Way of the Fool journal if that will assist you…and to do it in whatever way and in whatever medium feels right. If you choose to record it at this time, pause the meditation until you're done.

Now that you feel complete with that interaction, step forward. Take another step. Then another, moving closer and closer to your Muse…until you step into your Muse, until you and your Muse become one, merging in a wondrous instant of creative union.

What does that feel like? What sensations or emotions run through you? What do you see? Sense? Hear? Intuit?

Breathe deeply into the merged entity you are and experience all there is to experience…feel all there is to feel…be all there is to be.

Take twenty seconds of clock time to experience this fully.

Now that you feel complete, step back and away from your Muse. Note any feelings or sensations that action sparks for you. As you step away, thank your Muse for assisting you today and allow your Muse to respond.

Before you leave this place, your Muse hands you a gift,

an expression of appreciation for having been freed into your life more consciously.

What is it?

Receive this gift and keep it with you.

Recall it, if you choose, every time you move into creator mode.

Now, turn back to the door — that special door — knowing you can return to this place at any time to meet with your Muse. All you need to do is remember how it felt to be here. All it takes is stillness. A quiet time. A quiet place, where you're free to envision, where it's safe to create.

Once more, you touch the door, it swings open and you step through...and back.

As you return to your starting place, you bring back with you all you sensed, all you saw and all you heard, felt and intuited.

You're bringing it back to your conscious awareness, remembering whatever, in this moment, it serves you to remember.

When you're ready, but only then, open your eyes, staying with all you experienced so you can express those experiences in whatever creative medium feels right.

Remember to create on the Muse Stream — without thinking or second-guessing, and censoring nothing as you free the voice of your Muse to live again in your creation.

The Steps

1. Break Old Rules to Break New Ground

2. Fire Up Your Passion

3. Be Daring!

4. Be Authentic

5. Dive Into the Mystery

6. Create in the Moment

7. Trust Your Muse

8. Free Your Creation

9. Strive for Excellence, Not Perfection

10. Commit to Your Passion

11. Reject Rejection

12. Celebrate Your Creations...and Your Creativity

12½. Embrace Your Vision

Step #1. Break Old Rules to Break New Ground

No rules. Just be with the moment.
Be in the moment. And trust.
Dialogues with the Divine:
Encounters with My Wisest Self

The realm of the imagination can be subject to
no laws, no statutes, no proclamations.

No rules.

It bows down to neither commandments nor edicts.

The realm of the imagination is sovereign.

The landscape of the imagination has no
predetermined roads, paths or trails,
nor has it any maps.

The landscape of the imagination is uncharted.

In this kingdom, you are explorer and trailblazer.
In this kingdom, there is no single right way or wrong
way to conceive, craft and complete any expression of
the heart...whatever it is, whatever it is about.

Whatever it is and whatever it is about,
it is the singular creation
of your unique heart and art.

No one else can conceive it.
No one else can express it.
Hence, no one else's ways of being
or doing can govern it.

The only right way is your way.
So refuse all rules and find your own way.

My Story

It's September 1967, a Wednesday morning early in my freshman year at Mount Royal High School. Expo '67, the world's fair marking Canada's centennial is winding down here in Montreal, and our English class has been assigned our first essay.

"Give me a thousand words on why Expo '67 is important for Canada," Mrs. Gold says. "You can write about which of your favorite pavilions is particularly significant or about what it means that so many people from all over the world are here in Montreal, or anything else on that theme."

My heart sinks. I hate writing.

"One more thing," she adds as the period bell clangs. "I want to see your outline."

I drag myself from my desk and trudge from Room 114. If there's one thing I hate more than writing essays, it's writing outlines.

That night, I roll one piece of blank paper after another into my portable typewriter, each sheet ultimately landing in a crumpled ball in the wastepaper basket by my desk. As hard as I try, I cannot map out the essay.

Thank God, we have a week for the assignment. I'll try again tomorrow.

I'm no more successful the next night or the night after. I have some ideas about how I would start the essay but no clue what would come next, let alone how I would get from there to the kind of conclusion Mrs. Gold told us she's looking for.

I love Expo. I have visited nearly all the pavilions since the fair opened in April. And there's hardly any white space left on the pages of my Expo passport, so filled are they with the stamps marking each of my visits. Between Expo and the other Centennial special events and activities, it's been a great year to be Canadian.

But what do I do with that?

Days pass. I make no progress.

It's now Monday night. I have written neither outline nor essay. Desperate, I roll a fresh sheet into the typewriter and begin pecking at the keyboard — not at the outline, at the essay. By midnight, I have a rough draft…and a rough outline I've crafted from the essay.

I polish both on Tuesday night and hand them in, on time, Wednesday morning.

Mission accomplished, even if, strictly speaking, that wasn't the mission.

A week later, Mrs. Gold returns our essays. Across the top of mine, in a neat red hand, are the words "Well Done!" followed by a giant "A."

The Way of the Fool

The Fool has no use for custom and convention…for maps, manuals or guidebooks. Others' paths are not hers, nor are others' ways of doing or being.

The Fool's journey is always an uncharted one, a series of leaps from the cliff of the known into the mysteries of the unknowable.

Just as each breath has never been breathed before, each step on the Way of the Fool is a unique one. Each moment arrives free of precedent. Each experience is its own creation and each creation, its own experience.

There are no footsteps to follow on the Way of the Fool. There are only fresh trails to blaze in a forest no one before has traversed. And although the trail thus blazed may one day become a path others follow, that is not the Fool's concern, goal or motivation. The Fool finds his own way and frees others to find theirs.

That is the Way of the Fool.

Your Story

Your Way of the Fool Journal

Have you started your Way of the Fool journal yet? If not, do it now, before you read on. Remember, there are no rules here. Remember, too, that there is no "right" way to answer this book's questions, complete its exercises or keep track of your thoughts and experiences as you explore the 12½ steps on the Way of the Creative Fool. So be like the Fool in this Step #1 and find your own way.

Whether you keep your journal in writing, with drawings or sketches, as a series of audio or video recordings or in a way that is unique to you, I promise that you will derive incalculable benefit from the experience.

For more journaling tips and suggestions, revisit "How to Use This Book" in the "Getting Started" section.

Quick Centering Meditation

Allow 5 minutes for this experience, longer if you plan further explorations in your Way of the Fool journal once you have completed the meditation.

This is an all-purpose meditation you can use anytime — when working with "The Way of the Creative Fool" and any of its steps, as part of your preparation for your day's work with the book, as a prelude to "Creating on the Muse Stream," below, or any creative work, or at any other time when a brief heart-centering exercise could help get you back on track.

Sit down — at your desk, in your favorite chair, in your favorite part of the garden, in your favorite park or on your favorite beach…wherever you feel comfortable, safe and inspired. Close your eyes, place your hands on your empty lap and breathe…in and out slowly, as slowly as you can, for a total of ten breaths.

Breathe more slowly with each breath, and feel your body relax more and more with each breath.

Feel each in-breath connect you to your Muse, to your higher self, wisest self, God self, or to whatever place within you that is your creative source, the source of your authentic expression. So breathe in. Slowly.

And as you breathe out, also slowly, let your exhalation flush all fear, doubt and anxiety from your mind and body. Let it flush all worldly concerns from your mind and body. Let it flush all stress and unease around creation and creativity from your mind and body. Let it flush all not-good-enoughs and not-creative-enoughs from your mind and body.

Focus now on your heart and breathe into that space, into that fire, that passion, that font of infinite creativity, infinite creative expression.

Breathe into your heart's vision for your creative expression and your creative life, however vague it might feel in this moment. Breathe into your truth.

Breathe in, breathe out and listen.

Listen for any messages or words of guidance — around creativity or anything else. If no messages or words of guidance come, that's okay. They may come next time, the time after, or not at all. This is not about rules or fixed outcomes. Nothing on *The Way of the Creative Fool* is about rules or fixed outcomes. It's about sitting in the silence and trusting that whatever needs to emerge from that silence will. It's about sitting in the silence and letting everything else go.

Continue breathing, in and out, for ten slow, deep breaths — for longer if that feels right. Again, this is not about rules.

It's about finding *your* way and learning to trust it.

When you feel ready, gently open your eyes and slowly move back into your day and into your creative life, carrying with you that deepened connection with your creative source, the source of your unique vision, the source of your most authentic, uncensored expression.

Try This

Open your Way of the Fool journal and jot down any notes about what you sensed and felt during the meditation…about what you saw and heard…about how you felt before the meditation and about how you feel now. If your journal isn't a written one, use whatever form or medium you feel called to use.

Meditation: No More Shoulds

Have your Way of the Fool journal handy to record your thoughts, feelings and impressions. Allow at least 35 minutes for this experience, longer if you plan further explorations in your journal once you have completed the meditation.

Revisit "Getting Started" for tips on how best to use all this book's meditations, visualizations and meditative journeys.

Relax. Close your eyes. Adjust your position to get as comfortable as you can.

Take a deep breath in...then let it go. Another, deeper... and let that one go. And a third, deeper still...and let that one go, expelling as much breath as you can from as deep a place as you can.

Now, let your breath return to normal, even as you hold your focus on it.

As you inhale, breathe in calm and quiet. Total relaxation. As you exhale, breathe out fears, fatigue, stress.

As you inhale, breathe in inner peace. Total surrender. As you exhale, let your shoulders drop.

Can you drop them some more? We carry all our musts, have-tos and shoulds in our shoulders. Picture the word "shoulder" and note how much of that word is made up of the word "should."

When we hunch our shoulders, we hold in all those shoulds, all those musts, all those have-tos.

"I should create this"; "I have to create this way"; "I must create in a way that does not offend"; "I should be doing this or that instead of working on my creative projects"; "I should be working on my creative projects instead of doing this or that."

In holding on to those shoulds, musts and have-tos, we enable and empower them to disrupt and block our freest creative flow...our freest *life* flow.

So as you let your shoulders drop, let some of those shoulds, musts and have-tos fall away.

How does that feel?

Now, let your shoulders drop again, so more of those shoulds, musts and have-tos can fall away.

Can you feel them sliding off...all those shoulds, musts and have-tos? Can you feel them sliding away? If you can't, or even if you can, let your shoulders drop one more time. This time, if you need to, give those shoulds, musts and have-tos a gentle nudge.

Not a nudge of frustration, anger or resentment. Let it truly be a gentle one, of gratitude, for all the ways those shoulds, musts and have-tos have served and protected you over the years. And they have.

They served you once and they served you well. But you don't need them anymore. Now, they are little more than an old habit that is getting in the way of newer, healthier habits. So give them that gentle nudge…that gentle, grateful nudge.

How does that feel? Lighter, right?

The problem with shoulds, musts and have-tos, though, is that we always have an unending supply of them. As one falls away, another — one rooted, perhaps, more deeply in our past…maybe all the way back to earliest childhood — emerges to take its place, weighing us down all over again.

You needn't be weighed down anymore. Not by more recent shoulds, musts and have-tos. Not by older ones. Not by the absolute oldest ones.

Imagine, if you will, that you have two waterfalls, one resting on each shoulder. Imagine, too, that the clear, cleansing waters of those waterfalls are continually flushing the shoulds, musts and have-tos not solely from your conscious mind but from your unconscious mind.

As long as you keep dropping your shoulders, as long as your shoulders are not hunched, the waters of those waterfalls can cascade freely off you — off your physical body, out of your emotional body and out of your energy field — washing away all those shoulds, all those musts, all those have-tos.

Here's the other problem with shoulds, musts and have-tos. The bigger problem. When we let shoulds, musts and have-tos run our lives and take charge of our creativity, they muzzle us. Always. They censor us. Always. They force us to second-guess. Everything.

Shoulds, musts and have-tos stop us from being original. They stop us from being authentic. They stop us from expressing the deepest truths of our deepest heart. They stop us from finding our own way. They stop us from being creative.

How are your shoulders now? If you still feel some tightness, focus on your breath again, and send your breath into your shoulders. Let your breath be like the skilled fingers of a massage therapist, working out any knots, loosening your muscles, relaxing any residual tension.

Imagine those waterfalls again. See the waters cascading freely off you again.

Now, though, look into those waters. Look into those waters and see some of the shoulds, musts and have-tos. Which can you identify? Which can you see? Which are flowing away freely? Which seem stuck?

Acknowledge the ones that are flowing away freely. Acknowledge them, and thank them for their service as you let them go.

And if, among the ones that feel sluggish or stuck, there are any you can identify — or can see but not exactly identify — thank them too. Thank them and invite them to move on, to move over the waterfall's ledge, off your shoulders and away.

If they resist your invitation, that's okay. Don't force anything. Simply come back to this meditation another day and try again. As often as is helpful.

That's true of all the meditations, visualizations and meditative journeys on this Way of the Creative Fool. Each experience of each one will take you deeper. So don't hesitate to repeat this or any of them.

In a few moments, I'm going to invite you to open your eyes and write about your experiences in your Way of the Fool journal. Write about the waterfalls. Write about whatever shoulds, musts and have-tos you have been able to identify, even those you can't yet let go. Write about why you can't let them go. And write about how it feels to let go those you are able to release on the waters of your waterfalls.

As you write, use the Muse Stream technique I introduced you to in the "Your Muse and You" section. As a reminder, that means writing without thinking and without stopping to edit, second-guess or censor.

If you prefer, use a different creative medium to describe and release whatever shoulds, musts and have-tos you experienced in this mediation. Draw them. Sing them. Move to them. Improvise them. Cook them. Garden them. Craft them. Regardless, don't let any shoulds, musts or have-tos get in the way of your deepest, most heartful and heartfelt expression.

Journal/create for 20 or 30 minutes, longer if that's what you're feeling.

For now, refocus on your breath. Refocus on your physical body. Refocus on whatever you're sitting on or lying on. Stretch your fingers. Move your hands. Move your feet. Squeeze and release your eyelids. And gently, very gently, open your eyes, open your journal and record your thoughts, feelings, impressions and experiences on the Muse Stream. Openly. Vulnerably. Without judgment. Without shoulds, musts or have-tos.

Creating on the Muse Stream

It's easy to lose sight of our voice, vision and style when we get invested in "rules" and orthodoxies...in how things are "supposed to be done"...in conventional tools and techniques...in what we've been taught...in what others are creating or how they're creating it. Without realizing what we're doing, we can find ourselves emulating others, rather than imagining and expressing work that's uniquely ours.

Back in "Your Muse and You," I introduced you to the Muse Stream, which I said would help you connect more authentically with your inner wisdom while journaling and while working with some *Way of the Creative Fool* exercises. However, the Muse Stream's benefits are not limited to journaling, or even to writing.

Let's look at how you can adapt the Muse Stream to any creative endeavor and, in this Step #1, how you can use it to help you find your creative path.

Whatever your creative genre, medium or form, these basic Muse Stream precepts always apply:

- Get out of your head and into your heart.

- Don't think. Don't structure. Don't plan.

- Listen for the voice of your Muse. Listen *to* the voice of your Muse. And create. Anything.

- As you get into a creative flow, go with your gut, your intuition, your inner knowing. Suspend all judgment, all censoring, all second-guessing.

- Keep going *without stopping*, even when you think you might be done. More often than not, that point when you're certain you're finished is the outer limits of your comfort zone. It's when we push past our comfort zone that we create our most powerful, compelling and evocative work.

- Don't think about outcomes or finished products; don't think about thinking about them.

- Give yourself permission to make mistakes, to be imperfect, to create something truly awful…to just have fun.

- Ideally, set a timer for 30, 45 or 60 minutes, depending on what's practical for your medium. Regardless, keep going for another 15 or 20 minutes or more once the timer goes off. As with pushing past your comfort zone, it's in those past-the-timer moments when we dive most deeply into the heart of our work.

- If it helps you surrender into a creative space, use the centering meditation earlier in this chapter, or any other meditation or meditative technique.

- Find yourself feeling stuck? Revisit the tips in "You and Your Muse." Focusing on your breath will nearly always restore your free flow, whatever you're working on or worrying about. Some of the other tips in "What's a Muse Stream" can also be adapted to most creative media.

In the explorations that follow, don't feel limited to one form of expression. Go with your primary creative outlet, of course. Then, once you're done, experiment with as many others as is practical. Finally, return to your primary outlet, noting any differences in your process and content in your Way of the Fool journal.

When we're challenged to connect with an easy flow in our primary genre, playing in others, especially on the Muse Stream, can bust open the dam of our hesitation and resistance.

Writers' Exploration

Follow the instructions in "Your Muse and You" and review the suggestions for what to do if you get stuck. Start anywhere and write *anything* — on the Muse Stream, of course — letting your words carry you where they will and letting them reveal to you what you need to know.

Photographers' Exploration

Take your camera or smartphone somewhere you have never been before, preferably to a type of setting or environment where you wouldn't normally go to shoot.

Shooting with a DSLR? For the purposes of this exercise, minimize distraction and downtime by taking only one lens with you; the one that's most versatile. If, like me, you tend to fuss with shutter and aperture settings, shoot automatic. If you must make adjustments, make them simple, and opt for aperture or shutter-speed priority mode. This isn't about the perfect shot. It's about expanding your vision.

Shooting with a smartphone? Ignore any manual settings your phone's camera app might offer. The same goes for scene settings and other options like pano.

The idea is to shoot on the Muse Stream; in other words, without taking time to frame or compose and without thinking, judging or second-guessing. This is not about photographing for quality, posterity, posting or sharing. It's about getting into an easy, natural flow, letting the camera lens be an extension of your eyes as you notice and capture what's around you — not from a place of adult discernment or perfectionism but from a place of childlike wonder and play.

Videographers' Exploration

Take the Photographers' Exploration and adapt it to video. Film, don't think. And have fun.

Visual Artists' Exploration

Whether you sculpt, etch, paint, draw, color or sketch

and whatever your medium, create without planning…or thinking.

If your medium is a portable one, consider following my suggestion to photographers and taking your kit somewhere you wouldn't normally go — for inspiration, even if you won't be using your surroundings as a subject.

Alternatively, experiment on your tablet with a drawing app and compatible electronic pencil. Or be a kid again and use your finger.

Whether you're working in studio, outdoors or somewhere else, start with your medium's version of a blank canvas, then paint, draw, sketch, sculpt or etch. Don't plan what to create. Don't think about what you will create. Instead, trust that your finished creation already exists, whole and complete, in its own realm.

Trust your finished work to know what it's about. Get out of the way, and let it reveal itself to you.

Artisans' and Crafters' Exploration

Take the Visual Artists' Exploration and adapt it to your medium. Create, don't think. And have fun.

Culinary Artists' Exploration

Set aside your favorite recipes and cookbooks and, instead, lay out some of your favorite ingredients, utensils and cookware.

Once you have them arrayed before you, close your eyes, get into a semi-meditative state, invite your intuitive self into the kitchen and listen. Listen to the ingredients. Listen for other ingredients not yet set out. Listen to your cookware and utensils. Listen to your inner chef. Listen to your intuition.

Don't think about results. Don't intellectualize about flavors or conventional combinations.

It doesn't matter whether what you end up with looks appetizing or tastes good. Instead, remember the toy oven you might have had as a kid, the mud pies you might have "baked" and the other concoctions you mindlessly threw together back then. Remember how much fun you had. Have that same fun now.

Performing Artists' Exploration

Whether you act, dance, sing, compose or play an instrument, improvise…in a genre or style that strays from your usual one. Your tone and delivery need not be appropriate for stage or screen. Your movement needn't be classical, or fluid. Your sounds needn't be melodic or familiar.

Be loud, jarring and dissonant, your movements and delivery broad and exaggerated. Or be subtle — whispery, nearly motionless and barely audible. Regardless, invite your inner child to take center stage and free your private performance from any identifiable form or structure. Get out of your head, be in the moment and let your expression be what *it* chooses to be, not what you think it ought to be…without worrying about others' reactions and without self-judgment, second-guessing or self-censorship.

Gardeners' Exploration

Your blank canvas is an empty plot, however tiny, that you can plant in from scratch. It can be a window box or a grouping of planters or pots. You have no outdoor space or room for a window box? Identify a suitable, plant-friendly spot inside your home.

When you have the time and patience, you can start with

seeds. For this exercise, however, head over to your favorite garden center and wander among the flowers, herbs and other plantings. Forget about what else you have already planted at home, outside or indoors. Don't think about what might fit in with your existing plantings. Don't worry too much about climate suitability; assume that if it's in your neighborhood garden center, it's reasonably appropriate.

As you stroll up and down the aisles, leave aside what you think you like. Instead, *listen*. Listen to the plants, to the ones that speak to you…that call out to you…that ask to go home with you…that ask to *not* go home with you. Get out of your head, and listen to your heart…to your inner gardener…to your intuition.

Keep listening once you get home — to what needs to be planted where, to what needs to be placed next to what.

This is not about making a pretty garden. This is about listening…and creating.

- *I didn't cover your creative medium or genre? Adapt any of the suggestions to the voice and call of your Muse.*

Ask Yourself These Questions…

Explore these questions in your Way of the Fool journal. Don't think about the answers, and don't feel as though you must answer each question individually if that doesn't feel right. It's okay to find your own way.

Let all your answers (or whatever single answer these questions trigger) emerge freely and honestly, writing them on the Muse Stream in a free-flowing, stream-of-consciousness way where appropriate.

- Where in my creative life am I letting other people's tools, techniques, teachings, definitions, methodologies or ways of doing things get in the way of discovering my own? Why am I making that choice? Those choices?

- Where in my creative life am I a follower when I could be an explorer and a trailblazer? How can I make that shift? What steps can I take in that direction today? What one step can I take right now?

- Where in my creative life am I being ruled by others' expectations for me? Whose expectations? Why do I feel attached to those expectations? What steps can I take to detach from at least one expectation? What one step can I take right now?

- Where in my creative life am I being ruled by my preconceptions of what an artist should be? Of what creative expressions in my medium should look like? Feel like? Sound like? Why do I feel attached to those preconceptions? What steps can I take to detach from at least one preconception? What one step can I take right now?

- How can I redefine creativity…not from any external "conventional" view, but from the inside out, from my heart not from my head?

- What can I do, starting today, to better chart my own course in my creative life?

The Way of the Dancing Fool

Although Montreal's Margie Gillis began dancing at age three, it was an emotional crisis precipitated five years later — when her parents split and her mother became critically ill — that ultimately sparked the unique style that would earn her international acclaim.

"I fell apart," she told *Dance Magazine* in 2019 of a breakdown so severe that all her hair fell out. (When it finally grew back, she vowed never to cut it. She didn't, and her waist-length hair would become a signature look emblematic of her quirky, freeform style.)

Gillis struggled for nearly a decade, frightened of everyone and of the world around her, and rarely dancing. Through that time, she said, "I watched my personality disintegrate and then reintegrate." When she recovered, it was with an unshakable certainty that her dancing would not only be emotionally healing for herself but for others as well.

"I wanted the work to be raw and natural, and I knew that while I could ask that of myself, it could be a vulnerable and frightening place [for other performers]. I began to create and perform solos."

It was those solos — "dancing from the inside out," as she has described her work — that would catapult her to meteoric fame, with sellout performances across Canada and around the world.

In her solo pieces, Gillis frees her movement to emerge from her breath and her vulnerability. That authenticity

and emotional honesty never fail to move her audiences…
often to tears.

Gillis didn't follow the traditional path to dance success. She is largely self-trained, did not rise through the ranks of an established company and never mastered formal technique. She blazed her own trail.

Margie Gillis dances the human experience. And she does it her way.

My Story: Coda

With that one freshman essay, written with neither plotting nor planning, I unknowingly took my first steps onto the Way of the Creative Fool. I couldn't see it then, of course, or for some time after, but the Muse Stream and everything I've taught and written in the years since had its genesis at age twelve with my decision to ditch that outline.[1]

Declaration

I, *your full name*, travel a creative path that is uniquely my own, one that is free of all shoulds, musts, have-tos, preconceptions and expectations — mine for myself as well as others' for me. As the Creative Fool that I am, I allow my heart and the voice of my Muse to guide me toward my most authentic creations. And so it is.

---

[1] Nearly sixty years have passed since that freshman class, so my essay experience probably didn't play out exactly as described, which is why I changed the name of my English teacher. Yet however it happened, I didn't outline that essay…or any that followed.

Step #2. Fire Up Your Passion

Find your passion and embrace it, passionately.
Then commit to your passion, unconditionally.
BIRTHING YOUR BOOK...EVEN IF YOU DON'T KNOW
WHAT IT'S ABOUT

Listen to what's inside you —
to the voice of your Muse,
which is the voice of your passion,
the voice of your intuition,
the voice of your discernment, and
the voice of your most authentic creations.

Ignore any and all voices that are critical,
censoring, second-guessing or judgmental —
those clamoring in your head as much as those
nagging at you from anywhere outside yourself.

Ignore, too, any arguments, rationalizations, claims or
debates that stem from fear or resistance —
others' or your own.

Focus only on your passion.

Where there is no passion, there is no heart.

Where there is no passion, there is no soul.
Where there is no passion, there is no truth.

Fire up your passion. Create what exhilarates you...
what electrifies you...what makes your blood race.

Create what you must create. Create what
only you can create.

Express your passion, fully and Fool-ly. Let passion
be your master...and your mastery.

My Story

IN THE DECADE before my novel *The MoonQuest* urged itself onto me (see "My Story: Coda I" in Step #7), I was a Toronto freelance writer and editor, producing articles, brochures, reports, speeches and advertising copy that reflected someone else's thoughts and ideas, and I did it to meet someone else's deadlines. I was being paid to write, for which I was grateful. But I rarely wrote anything I cared deeply about.

That I was writing at all was something of a miracle.

Growing up, I not only hated writing, I was certain I wasn't creative. And throughout my school years, all I wanted was to get through English class and its essay-writing burdens as quickly and painlessly as possible. (See "My Story" in Step #1.)

My Muse, however, had other plans for me. How else can you explain my first typewriter? A gift in my freshman year of high school, it wasn't a ubiquitous brand like Royal, Underwood or Smith-Corona. It was a little-known Hermes. Hermes, of course, was the Greek god of communication…and, thus, writers. And how can you explain why I agreed, a few years later, to take charge of publicity for the senior high school musical? It was so out-of-character for me to take on anything that involved not only writing but making my writing public that the me I am today still struggles to believe that the me I was then said yes.

I like to joke that my Muse tricked me into becoming a

writer, and that's how it began — with that typewriter and the publicity gig.

From high school musical press releases, I graduated to college musical press releases and, from there, to my first job: writing more press releases at a PR agency. My Muse upped the creative stakes at my next job, where I learned to write news and feature articles. It was that skill that, a few years later, transitioned me to the full-time freelancing I mentioned above.

My writer's story could have ended there, but it didn't… nor did the behind-the-scenes machinations of my Muse.

You see, I still refused to see myself as creative. A skilled artisan with words, perhaps. But certainly not creative.

That changed one Monday morning during a simple water-cooler conversation. I was working in Toronto as an in-house freelance editor when a staffer corralled me.

"I've just taken this fantastic creative writing workshop," she gushed, unknowingly channeling my Muse. "You've got to take it."

In a moment as out-of-character as the one when I agreed to run publicity for my high school *Hello, Dolly!*, I said yes.

That "yes" triggered an astounding transformation.

Thanks to the workshop, I found myself writing from my heart instead of from my head. I found myself writing *my* stories instead of others'. And I discovered a love of storytelling I never knew I had.

After so many years of running from my creativity, I had embraced it. I had fired up my passion and, to borrow from mythologist Joseph Campbell, I was following my bliss. Finally.

The Way of the Fool

The Fool need not fire up his passion, for passion is already the fire that feeds his every action, every undertaking, every creation…the fire that feeds his soul. Thus, nothing about each breath and each waking moment of the Fool's life is not steeped in passion.

The passions of the Fool are neither fleeting nor superficial. Rather, they are core to her very essence, rising from the heart of her beingness as the most authentic expressions of her deepest connection with Source and her most faithful relationship with her Essential Self.

Living his passion is the sole option for the Fool because in his world and world view, no other options exist. Passion is the only possible choice…so there is no choice. There is only passion.

When you live your passion and free your passion to fuel every aspect of your life, you walk the Way of the Fool.

Your Story

Exploration I • The Right Stuff

There are many good ideas out there — ideas for books and screenplays…for songs and symphonies…for pictures and paintings…for gardens and goulash…for everything and anything creative.

In fact, there are so many good ideas out there that it's difficult to avoid them. They're all over the media. They're all over the internet. And your friends, colleagues, parents, spouses, siblings and teachers have been offering them up to you for years. Your logical mind too.

Yet there's a difference between a good idea and the right idea, between an idea that is anyone's for the taking and one that is uniquely yours, one that speaks to your singular gifts and your unique passions. It's those passions, those "right" ideas, that fuel your creative fire.

Yes, good ideas can add kindling to the fire. But kindling flares up swiftly and burns out just as swiftly if the fire isn't fed with something more substantial.

That "something more substantial" is your passion…is your *right* idea.

So before you launch into a creative frenzy, ask yourself: Is this where my passion lies? Is this the call of my Muse, the creation that's uniquely mine? Or could this be anyone's? Is this another good idea, or is this the right idea for me?

Anyone can take a good idea and give it shape and substance. Some can do it better than you, some not as well.

No one can take the idea that sings to your soul and perform the kind of alchemy on it that you can. Only you can transform that right idea into the one-of-a-kind gem it longs to be. That is why it, through your Muse, called to you…chose you.

Accept that you were chosen. Perform your magic. Express your passion. Take that right idea and sing your soul into it. Do it. Now.

Try This

Move into a meditative space, a place of deep connection. Take a few deep breaths in and out. When you're relaxed, pick up your pen and write on the Muse Stream in your Way of the Fool journal for 20 minutes, using this as your key phrase: "My Muse calls on me to create…"

After You've Journaled

Were you surprised? Did you discover a new direction? Confirmation of an existing one? Now, take what you discovered or had confirmed and create…on the Muse Stream.

Meditation: Create from the Heart

Have your Way of the Fool journal handy to record your thoughts, feelings and impressions. Allow at least 25 minutes for this experience, longer if you plan further explorations in your journal once you have completed the meditation.

My studio recording of "Create from the Heart," nearly identical to this meditation, is available for download or streaming[1] as part of "The Voice of the Muse Companion: Guided Meditations for Writers," where it's titled "Write from the Heart."

Revisit "Getting Started" to find out how to access the recording, as well as for tips on how best to use this book's meditations, visualizations and meditative journeys.

Relax. Close your eyes. Focus on your breath. Breathe deeply. In and out. In and out. In and out. Continue to breathe, in and out, breathing in relaxation, breathing in freedom…allowing any stress, anxiety or tightness to relax into freedom on your breath.

Listen to the rhythm of your heart. Feel it beating. Feel it pumping life throughout your body. Down into your abdomen, groin, legs, feet and toes. Up into your neck and shoulders, your mouth, nose and ears. Your eyes. Feel its power in your arms, hands and fingers. The hands you create with.

The hands of creation.

Feel that life force circulate freely, spiraling throughout your body, creating patterns and shapes, colors and sounds.

Listen to the rhythm of that life force centered in your heart. And in that rhythm, through that rhythm, listen for the voice of your Muse.

What does it mean to create from the heart? Is it physically possible? Can your fingers reach back in on themselves, travel up your arms, past your elbows and shoulders, then down your chest to touch that central mind that, were it truly in charge, would revolutionize your creativity, your creative expression and your life?

For, yes, your heart is your central mind — a mind more powerful, life-fulfilling and life-affirming than

---

[1] Search the relevant site/store for "Mark David Gerson write from the heart"

your brain, as powerful and magical a piece of machinery as that is.

Yet that's what it is: a piece of machinery. A wondrous, miraculous machine, but a machine nonetheless.

When we let machines take charge of our creativity, when we let machines take charge of our lives, the result is mechanical, soulless, spiritless.

We don't touch others at a deep level when we connect mind-to-mind, though that connection is a powerful and important one. We touch others at a deep level when we connect heart-to-heart.

So let your fingers reach back in on themselves. See them traveling through your arms...on the inside, not the outside.

See them reaching past your wrists and up your forearms, past your elbows and up to your shoulders. Let them stop there for a moment and, from their place deep inside your muscles, bone and tissue, let them massage and caress the tension from, in and around those shoulders.

Now let your fingers continue down to your heart — the organ on the left side of your chest and the chakra or energy center in the middle of your chest.

Let your fingers continue down. As they do, let them clear away any cobwebs, let them unlock any doors or gates, let them dissolve any walls or barriers, let them move in gently and caress that place of love with love. Let the energy of that love, of that place of heart-centeredness, fill your fingertips.

Let the memory of all the love you have experienced, all the loving experiences you have lived, let that memory fill your fingertips so that when, in a few moments, you return them to your creative expression, whatever that creative expression is, that love will infuse every act, action and moment that flows from them, from that connection to your heart that is always there and can always be reignited.

Continue to breathe, to breathe deeply, as you open your heart and clear away and free all that has been scarred, barricaded and bottled up. Breathe in the clarity. Breathe in the focus. Breathe in the love, the self-love, the love of your heart, your Muse, your creations.

Continue to breathe, in and out, in and out, for a few more moments.

In and out.

In and out.

In and out.

Slowly.

Deeply.

Fully.

As you breathe, listen. Focus your attention on your heart. Focus all your attention on your heart. In this moment, let nothing exist but your heart.

Listen to it. Listen for its voice, for the voice of your Muse as expressed through your heart. Listen to your heart. Still yourself and listen.

Your heart has a message for you. A word, a phrase… many words, many phrases. As you continue to focus and listen, you will hear it.

Clearly.

Once you hear it, open your eyes and write what you hear in your Way of the Fool journal.

Continue listening and writing, listening and writing, recording all you hear or sense, in this moment.

And now this one.

And now this one.

If you hear or sense nothing at this time, don't judge yourself. Simply launch your journey using this key phrase: "My heart speaks to me of…"

In either case, write on the Muse Stream, remembering

to keep your pen moving across the page or your fingers dancing across the keyboard, letting it be the medium through which your heart speaks to you.

Write your heart words until you sense completion.

Then hold the silence for a few breaths longer, open to anything new your heart has to say.

After You've Journaled

Take the messages of your heart and apply them directly to your creativity — to an existing project or a new one, in your usual medium or a new one. Whatever your project or medium, remember to create on the Muse Stream.

After You've Created

How was this creative session different from what you experienced in "Creating on the Muse Stream" in Step #1? In process? In content? In emotional response? In resistance? Take a few minutes and note those differences, along with how the experience made you feel, in your Way of the Fool journal.

Exploration II • Feeling Stuck or Blocked?

If you're feeling stuck, ask yourself whether the project that's going nowhere is one that excites and impassions you, one that fires you up more than anything else you could be creating. Is it the right idea for you right now? Or is it another good idea that anyone could take on?

If you have lost the excitement (or never had it) and cannot rekindle (or find) your enthusiasm, consider that this may not be the best project for you at this time...or ever.

Lack of passion is a guaranteed recipe for stuckness.

Passion, on the other hand, will always fuel your creativity.

A wrong idea isn't necessarily wrong for all time. But if it's wrong for right now, let it go and free yourself to create what's right. For you. Right now.

Ask Yourself These Questions

Explore these questions in your Way of the Fool journal. Don't think about the answers, and don't feel as though you must answer each question individually if that doesn't feel right. It's okay to find your own way.

Let all your answers (or whatever single answer these questions trigger) emerge freely and honestly, writing them on the Muse Stream in a free-flowing, stream-of-consciousness way where appropriate.

- How do I feel about the project that is going nowhere, the project that is making me feel blocked? Does it fire me up? Is it something I care passionately about? Or is it merely another good idea?

- If it fires me up, what's holding me back? How can I use *The Way of the Creative Fool* to reinspire myself? What else can I do to rekindle my passion?

- If it's a good idea but not the right idea, why have I devoted so much energy to it? Can I let it go and move on? What right idea can replace it?

The Way of the Passionate Fool

For years, art director Sandra Reichl had a passion for people who lived their passion. In fact, she was so inspired and fascinated by them that she started a list. She called it "Inspiring People" and added to it every time she came across one of their stories.

Reichl didn't care what her inspiring people were passionate about, and didn't limit her list to particular fields of endeavor. Anyone from artists to entrepreneurs could be on it, as long as their journey struck a chord with her. "Some," she told the *Gents Cafe* newsletter, "found their passion in an unexpected way. Others had made bold, one-hundred-eighty-degree career shifts."

For nearly a decade, it remained nothing more than a growing catalog of names. Then one day, when Reichl discovered that she had collected nearly a hundred inspiring people, she realized she was at a crossroads: She could keep adding names until her list reached two hundred or five hundred or a thousand, or she approach some of these men and women to hear their stories first-hand.

She decided on the latter. She picked ten names and reached out for interviews. Seven agreed, and those first seven became the foundation for a new magazine she titled *A Passion Thing*.

That was in 2019.

Today, and now joined by co-editor and business partner Karin Novozamsky, Reichl publishes *A Passion Thing* twice a year from editorial offices in Austria. And Reichl's passion for people who live their passion is stronger than ever.

She says the magazine's mission has always been clear: to uncover the stories of inspiring people who have turned their passion into something bigger — a venture, a career, a sustainable business. "It was never meant to be just a hobby magazine. The idea was to explore how passion can be transformed into a way of life, not just something you do on the side."

What's passion for Sandra Reichl? Passion, she says, is about making every day meaningful, even the challenging ones. It's about not giving up when times are tough. Sometimes, it's exploring different potential passions to discover what truly drives you. And sometimes, it's leaving old passions behind as you move into new ones.

"Passion," she says, "is a journey, not a fixed destination."

My Story: Coda

Unlike in my twenties when, as a freelance journalist, my writing was skilled and craftsmanlike and written from the surface, my current creations rise from profound, gut-wrenching inner places that challenge me as little else in my life ever has. In metaphysical terms, they are "energy activations" that force me to face my deepest fears and impel me to trust more fully and surrender more absolutely than I sometimes believe possible.

All my creative projects come from that place... including *The Way of the Creative Fool*. I expected this to be among the easiest of my books to produce, calling as it does on all I've written about creativity over the years. Yet it has found ways to test me.

The writing itself hasn't been difficult, thanks to the Muse Stream. What pushes and stretches me is something deeper: the tectonic shifts of inner revolution — outer, too, sometimes — that are inevitable byproducts of this type of journey.

Even on those book-writing days when I grumble and grouse and raise my voice to the heavens with a *God, I wish I was finished!*, I must acknowledge the real reason I write, the real reason I create. It's to experience those tectonic shifts, to uncover hidden depths, to discover what it is I believe, to remember all I have forgotten.

I could insist that I write to inspire, engage, impassion, motivate and touch others...and that would be true. I do wish for my books to accomplish all those things. But the only way I can do that for others is if I first do it for myself. How? By surrendering to the leaps of faith that this journey of creating from the heart always demands.

Declaration

I, *your name*, align myself with the fullness and Fool-ness of my passion, freeing the depth and richness of that passion to influence and inform everything I create and every aspect of my creative life. And so it is.

Step #3. Be Daring!

Commit today to taking more risks, to going out on a limb. Commit to letting yourself be judged... and letting it be okay.
WRITER'S BLOCK UNBLOCKED: SEVEN SUREFIRE WAYS TO FREE UP YOUR WRITING AND CREATIVE FLOW

Creative artists are innovators.
Creative artists are trailblazers.
Creative artists journey off the edge of the earth,
to those places where maps of old warned,
"Here, there be dragons."

Creative artists dare to create
what only they can create,
in the way that only they can create it.

Creative artists dare to be bold.

Dare to be bold.
Dare to be original.
Dare to be you.

My Story

FOR YEARS, ONE OF my closet fantasies was to be a singer. Unfortunately, I was so shy and self-conscious about my voice that I never even tried to join my high school glee club. Still, I did manage to summon up the courage to audition for a singing role in the school's production of *Hello, Dolly!* (I didn't get it), an uncharacteristic act of daring that continues to astound me.

It would take twenty-six years before I dared act on that fantasy a second time. The result was nothing I could have expected or imagined.

I was living in Toronto, deep into a period of spiritual expansion and emotional healing, when I saw an ad for voice classes in *Now*, the city's alternative weekly.

Figuring it was time to do something about my singing fantasy, I called the number in the ad. It wasn't easy to dial that number. I was no less self-conscious about my voice at forty-two than I had been at sixteen. So I was relieved to discover that the ad wasn't for singing classes. The "voice classes" were for actors.

I opened my mouth to say, "Not interested."

Instead, I heard myself say, "Sign me up."

Two weeks later, as I drove across town to the Actors' Equity studio, I wondered why I'd said yes. Sure, instructor David Smukler was one of Canada's top voice coaches. But what did that have to do with me?

For five weeks, I showed up and gamely did the vocal

and physical exercises with my fellow students, all actors. It was strange but fun. Challenging too. Still, it wasn't singing. Why *was* I there?

Then, for our final exercise, we were each assigned a Shakespeare sonnet and told to memorize and perform it for the class using a Method-like technique. In other words, we were to find our life and experience in Shakespeare's words and speak it from that place. Mine was Sonnet 43.

As I read and reread Shakespeare's centuries-old words of yearning and absence, it didn't take me long to connect them with my father, a man who had barely acknowledged my existence, then died before my fourteenth birthday.

Method actors are trained to harvest their emotional life in ways that bring authenticity to their roles. They're also trained to not let that connection interfere with the acting job.

"Feel what you feel," David instructed us, "but those feelings are there to fuel you, not to take over your performance."

They took over mine. Although my solo rehearsals were as on-the-mark as a non-actor could make them, as soon as I opened my mouth in front of the class, the dam broke. It took all the control I could muster to make it through the fourteen lines without sobbing.

For years, I had claimed emotional detachment from the circumstances surrounding my paternity. After all, why would I mourn a father I had never experienced? Yet telling my story through Shakespeare's words brought me close to an emotional truth that until that moment I had never been able to touch.

I have never been able to identify what shut me down emotionally and creatively as a child. If it was some long-ago word or act, I don't remember it. But what if it wasn't something said, but something left unsaid? Can the absence of a father's loving words be as numbing to a child as the presence of harsh words? What if my father's absence was a presence so palpable that it absented me from myself? What if in feeling devalued, however unconsciously, by my father, I had so devalued myself that I erased magic and memory from my being and creativity from my life?

When I signed up for David's class, a decision more daring than had it been about singing, I didn't know why I was doing it. It certainly wasn't to learn how to act. By the end of that class, I knew why I was there: to dare how to feel — in my creativity as much as in the rest of my life.

The Way of the Fool

The Fool does not see herself as bold, dauntless or audacious. Nor would he describe himself as brave, courageous or fearless…or valiant, intrepid or heroic. Or daring. Yet she is all these, and more.

Not by intentioned choice. Not through deliberate acts of derring-do. Not because he thrives on danger or seeks out risk.

Rather, the Fool listens only to her heart and acts on its urgings alone — wherever they take her, whatever they call on her to do, however they call on her to be. Wherever, whatever, however, the Fool responds accordingly…and unquestioningly, with neither apology nor explanation and without heed to others' creeds, cautions or counsel.

The Fool does not debate, decide or deliberate. The Fool does not compute, calibrate or calculate. The Fool weighs neither options nor outcomes. He simply is, each breath an affirmation of the sovereignty of the heart.

That is the Way of the Fool.

Your Story

Meditation: Into the Heart of Daring

Have your Way of the Fool journal handy to record your thoughts, feelings and impressions. Allow 20 to 30 minutes for this experience, longer if you plan further explorations in your journal once you have completed the meditation.

Revisit "Getting Started" for more tips on how best to use this book's meditations, visualizations and meditative journeys.

Relax. Close your eyes. Get into a comfortable position. Let your shoulders drop. And drop some more. Take a few deep breaths, in and out, in and out, breathing in calm and quiet, breathing out fears, fatigue, stress. Breathing in peace and centeredness, breathing out the worries of the moment, the anxieties of the day.

You're relaxed but alert. Awake and aware. Moving into a quiet place. A deep place. A place of freedom, vision and awakening. A place of courage. A place of movement. A place of creativity. A place of daring.

Fear will always stop us from moving forward in our creative lives, if we let it. Fear of success. Fear of failure. Fear of judgment. Fear of criticism. Fear of ridicule. Fear of shame. Fear of praise. Fear of what we might discover about ourselves through our creations. Fear of what we might reveal to others through our creations. Fear of consequences we can imagine. Fear of consequences we dare not imagine. Fears we can't identify. Fears we don't realize we have.

It is fear that holds us back from making the bold, daring choices that awaken our creative passion, that ignite our creative fire. It is fear that holds us back from taking creative risks…from taking creative chances. With our work. In our lives.

As you contemplate that and what that might mean in your creative life, breathe into your heart. Your heart is your place of courage. Your heart is your place of daring.

It's no accident that the word "courage" and all the Romance language words for "heart" sound similar and likely come from the same Latin root, *cor*.

Coeur in French. *Cuore* in Italian. *Corazón* in Spanish.

Your heart is your place of courage.

Yet courage is not the same as fearlessness. Courage is your ability to not let yourself be paralyzed by your fear, to act in spite of your fear, to move through and past your fear to the place where your destiny awaits you. More often than not, if not always, you must take a chance to get there. You must make a daring choice. You must take a leap of faith. Just as the Fool does.

In a moment, I am going to ask you a series of questions. Simple questions. When I ask them, I don't want you to think about your answer. I want you to let whatever answer first bubbles up into your conscious awareness be the answer. Be *your* answer. It may not be an answer you want to hear. It doesn't have to make sense. If this is not your first time doing this meditation, it probably won't be the same answer you got last time, though it could be.

There are no right or wrong answers to these questions. Whatever answers you get are the right ones for right now. The perfect ones for right now.

Your answer could be a single word or phrase. It could

be a couple of sentences. It could be a brief paragraph. Keep it short and simple if you can. We will look at your answers in greater depth in the Exploration that follows this meditation.

Here's the first question...

In this moment, what are you most afraid of when it comes to your creativity, to your creative life? Again, in this moment, what are you most afraid of when it comes to your creativity, to your creative life?

Open your eyes for a moment and jot down your brief answer in your Way of the Fool journal. Pause your meditation or your recording of it if you need to, and start again when you're ready.

In this moment, what are you most afraid of?

Remember, there will be an opportunity to journal about your answer in the Exploration that follows this meditation. For now, close your eyes, refocus on your breath and on your heart and answer this next question.

Remember to go with your first thought. Second thoughts are doubting, self-censoring thoughts. First thoughts carry you to the heart of your truth and the truth of your heart.

Here's the next question...

What daring action or choice in your creative life are you hesitating about making at this time?

It could be directly related to your creative expression... its form, its medium, its content. Or it could be indirectly related.

Maybe it has something to do with letting others experience your work, or with some other aspect of freeing it into the world. Maybe it has to do with steps you're reluctant to take, with individuals you're hesitant to reach out to.

Whatever it is for you, what daring action or choice in

your creative life are you hesitating about making at this time in your life?

Once again, open your eyes for a moment and jot down your word or phrase or sentence — whatever first comes to mind. Pause your meditation or your recording of it if necessary.

What daring action or choice in your creativity or your creative life are you hesitating about taking at this time?

Again, you will have an opportunity to journal about your answer in the Exploration that follows this meditation. For now, gently close your eyes and focus on your breath and on your heart as you answer this final question. It's a two-part question.

Here's the first part…

How would your life be different if you made that daring choice? If you took that daring action? There could be one answer to this question or multiple answers. But focus first on the one that leaps immediately to mind. How would your life be different if you made that daring choice or took that daring action?

Here's the second part…

How would your life be different if you made that daring choice or took that daring action and your "gamble" paid off? Again, there could be multiple answers to this, but focus as always on first thoughts. How would your life be different if you made that daring choice or took that daring action and your "gamble" paid off?

One final time, open your eyes long enough to jot down your quick answer to each of this question's two parts, pausing your meditation or recording if necessary.

The first part: How would your life be different if you made that daring choice or took that daring action?

And the second part: How would your life be different

if you made that daring choice or took that daring action and your "gamble" paid off?

In the Exploration that follows this, we'll look more closely at all your answers. For now, close your eyes and return your attention to your breath, to your heart, to this moment.

Focus on your breath, letting your breath deepen again as you slowly inhale…and exhale. Inhale…and exhale.

Inhale…and exhale.

As you breathe, breathe into the heart of your courage and the courage of your heart. Into the heart of your vision and the vision of your heart. Into the heart of your truth and the truth of your heart. Into the heart of your daring and into the daring of your heart. Into the heart of your Fool-ishness and into the Fool-ishness of your heart.

Let the breath of your heart and the heart of your breath enfold and embrace you. Feel its love. Feel its gentleness. Feel its peace. Also feel its fire, its passion, its ferocity. And know that when you create from your heart on the Way of the Creative Fool, you are always safe. Always.

Now, as you let your breath return to normal, allow your focus to stray from this meditative experience to your immediate surroundings. To whatever you're sitting or lying on, for example. To whatever sounds or smells might be drifting toward you. To the touch of your clothes against your body. Become more aware of your body by wiggling your toes…by stretching your fingers…by gently moving your head up and down and from side to side.

When you're ready, but only when you're ready, slowly open your eyes and rejoin your day, ready to explore all the awareness this experience has gifted you, knowing that its gifts will not end with this meditation but will continue to manifest and unfold in the days, hours and weeks ahead.

Exploration • I

It's time to explore your answers to the questions I posed to you as part of the "Into the Heart of Daring" meditation. If you haven't experienced the meditation yet, answer them now; they're repeated below. If you answered the questions during the meditation but didn't do the meditation today, answer them again…to see if your answers have changed. If you are doing this Exploration immediately after the meditation, skip to the "Deep Dive."

The Questions

Keep your answers brief, down to a word or phrase, a sentence or two, or a short paragraph. We will explore your answers in greater depth in the "Deep Dive."

Remember to let the first response that leaps to mind be your answer to each of these questions. Do your best to not second-guess yourself or to let your fearful or skeptical mind censor you. Answer from your heart.

- In this moment, what am I most afraid of when it comes to my creativity, to my creative life?

- What daring action or choice in my creative life am I hesitating about making at this time?

- How would my life be different if I were to make that daring choice or take that daring action?

- How would my life be different if I were to make that daring choice or take that daring action and my "gamble" paid off?

Deep Dive

Take each of your answers individually or all of them together and explore them in more detail in your Way of the Fool journal. Dive deeply into those answers and into what underlies them, and let your thoughts, impressions and feelings emerge freely and honestly, writing them on the Muse Stream where appropriate.

There are no right or wrong answers to these questions. Whatever answers you get are the right ones for right now. The perfect ones for right now.

Return to these questions again and again as you move through *The Way of the Creative Fool*, and note how your answers change over time. Or how they don't.

If writing isn't your journaling medium of choice, express your answers to these questions in whatever creative way you feel called to. Just as there are no right or wrong answers, there is no right or wrong way to express those answers.

Exploration • II

Use the following key phrases to kick off your journaling. Give yourself at least 15 minutes to write from each. Write on the Muse Stream and, if you find yourself getting stuck, use one of the techniques I describe in "The Muse and You." Keep writing until the 15 minutes are up, longer if you're in the flow and want to keep going. Don't feel as though you must work with all three phrases in a single sitting.

- I am ready to dare by…
- I am ready to create boldly by…
- I am ready to step out of my comfort zone in my creativity by…

Exploration • III

Explore these questions in your Way of the Fool journal but don't think about the answers. Let your answers emerge freely and honestly, writing them on the Muse Stream in a free-flowing, stream-of-consciousness way.

- Where can I plumb the emotions and experiences that I share with all humanity to create what I wouldn't before have dared to create?
- Where can I plumb those same emotions and experiences to go deeper in my creative expression?

Creating on the Muse Stream

Revisit "Creating on the Muse Stream" from Step #1, and repeat the exercise.

When You're Finished…

How was this creative session different from others you have experienced? In process? In content? In emotional response? In resistance? Take a few minutes and note those differences, along with how the experience made you feel, in your Way of the Fool journal.

The Way of the Designing Fool

When the winning design for the Vietnam Veterans Memorial was unveiled in May 1981, the outrage was immediate...and deafening.

Yale architecture student Maya Lin's daring vision was for a partly subterranean V-shaped wall of polished black granite into which would be carved the names of those who were killed or missing in action. Simple, stark and somber, it bore no resemblance to traditional war memorials with their figurative representations of military heroes.

Critics attacked it as ugly, shameful and unpatriotic, dubbing it "a black gash of shame and sorrow" and describing it as "a nihilistic slab of stone," "an open urinal" and "a monument to defeat, one that spoke more...to a nation's guilt than to the honor of...[its] veterans."

They didn't stop there. Lin, they insisted, couldn't possibly understand either America or the war; she was too young, too female, too Asian.

Many demanded the project be scrapped, and two prominent financial backers withdrew their support once they saw the design. Secretary of the Interior James Watt delayed issuing a building permit in the face of all the opposition.

In the end, of course, the Memorial was built. And although a more traditional sculpture — a statue of three soldiers with a flag — was added to the site as a compromise, it could never compete with the wall.

What was once condemned as disrespectful and inappropriately daring today attracts well over five million visitors a year. Many can be seen weeping as they run their fingers over the letters that spell out the names of sons, brothers and friends[1]. Often, they leave flowers and other mementos. If they are lucky, they leave having found some measure of resolution. Even tourists with no direct connection to the conflict can't help but be deeply moved by the sober memorial and its tens of thousands of names.

---

[1] Among the Memorial's more than fifty-eight thousand men's names are the names of the eight military servicewomen, all nurses, who died in Vietnam.

My Story: Coda I

A few months after David Smukler's class, I reread the latest draft of my first novel, *The MoonQuest*, which I hadn't looked at since before my experience with Sonnet 43. To my surprise, parts of it felt emotionally flat.

After weeks of frustrating attempts at fixes, I recalled a technique I teach in my fiction-writing workshops. Basically, you get into a meditative space, summon your characters and ask them questions. Then you use my Muse Stream technique to free-write their answers.

So one afternoon, I imagined first Fynda, then Yhoshi, then Garan sitting across from me at my kitchen table, and I asked each in turn to tell me more about themselves and their lives.

What emerged was graphic, grueling and brutal... the most gripping and emotionally raw scenes I had ever written.

Fynda shared a nightmare where she experienced a vicious assault. Yhoshi told of a savage raid on his family's village. Garan spoke of how fear had disfigured him.

At first, I hated what I had written. I also hated myself for having written it. How could I, a man of gentle spirit, have written such grim violence?

Thing is, when we write fiction from the deepest places in our soul, as I had done with *The MoonQuest*, every character is, in some way, an expression of us. That meant I was as much Fynda's attacker as I was Fynda, as much the marauding King's Men as the innocent villagers, as much Garan's terror as my own.

Just because I was easygoing and nonviolent didn't mean I lacked a dark side. Far better to be open to it than repress it. Far better to release it onto the page than act it out. Far better to share it than hide it.

Without Sonnet 43 — and without the daring choices that got me there and kept me there — I could never have touched the emotional depth that freed me to write those scenes…scenes I came to recognize as integral to *The MoonQuest*'s story and themes. Some two dozen books later, it remains some of my most powerful writing.

My Story: Coda II

What I gained from David Smukler's class also made it possible for me to write *Dialogues with Divine: Encounters with My Wisest Self*. To write it but not publish it…at least not right away. The journal-style memoir was so raw that it would take eighteen years and a whole lot more daring before I felt able to release it into the world.

Declaration

I, *your name*, dare to create everything that is in my heart to create, without second-guessing or censoring myself and without letting others' creeds, cautions or counsel get in the way. I listen for the voice of my Muse, I listen *to* the voice of my Muse, and I dare to be bold. And so it is.

Step #4. Be Authentic

Walk the earth naked, clothed only in your truth.
ACTS OF SURRENDER: A WRITER'S MEMOIR

Listen to your heart.
Still yourself and listen.

Listen to your heart
with neither judgment nor censorship.

Listen to your heart,
for all the truth that is, was or ever will be
resides there.

Listen to your heart and create from your heart.
Then free the authentic expressions of your heart
into the world to awaken other hearts.

Create from that place of authenticity.
Create from that place with courage and love.
Create from that place as though nothing
else matters, for nothing else does.

Create from that place,
and be the artist you are.

My Story

It's December 1997. I arrived in Sedona three months ago and have finally moved into my own place. But I'm feeling homesick for Toronto. The city was my on-and-off home for more than a dozen years…until I felt called to hit the road in what would turn out to be the three-month unplanned road odyssey that brought me here. So I pick up the phone and call KA'Ryna, a Toronto friend I met shortly before leaving town. KA'Ryna is a channel, though I have never experienced her work. I soon will.

We have barely begun chatting when she interrupts me. "I'm getting a message for you," she says. "Do you want to hear it?"

"Sure," I reply.

A few moments later, she's "in the zone."

"Do you know your vibrational name?" the group she is channeling asks through her.

"No." I'm unnerved. A local friend has been talking to me about spiritual names and the importance of using them in the world. "It's about being authentic," she keeps saying. I haven't mentioned those conversations to KA'Ryna.

"Would you like to?"

"Okay…"

"Would you like the name to come through KA'Ryna or directly to you?"

"Through me, please." Whatever is coming is certain

to be more empowering — maybe even authentic — if I experience it directly.

I sit in expectant silence. Nothing happens right away.

Then, it's as though I am feeling the name without physically hearing or seeing it. I try to shut my mind to it.

Despite my resistance, I sense first one letter...

A...

Then another...

K...

Then another...

H...

Then two more...

N... E...

"Okay," I cry silently. "I surrender!"

It's Akhneton, the name of an Egyptian pharaoh.

The audacity of it astounds me. The inappropriateness too. How can the name of an Egyptian pharaoh be the authentic vibrational name of a Jewish boy from Montreal?

Akhneton, I later discover, was a revolutionary monotheist who took on Egypt's powerful priestly class and decreed that the many gods of their Amenist tradition were now folded into a single god: Aten, the sun god. I learn, too, that Egyptologists believe Akhneton to have been Nefertiti's husband and Tutankhamen's father, and that the more traditional spelling is Akhenaten, pronounced Ah-keh-*NAH*-tin.

The pronunciation I sense with KA'Ryna is slightly different: *AHK*-na-tawn.

Next morning, in that hypnagogic state between waking and sleeping, I hear this phrase: "I am Akhneton Yoseyva, way-shower."

Yoseyva? What's that?

Whatever else it is, it's as bizarre as Akhneton. In the spirit of surrender, I decide that while I can accept

Akhneton Yoseyva as my authentic spiritual name, no one else need know about it. I will not use it out in the world.

My resolve lasts barely two weeks.

On New Year's Day 1998, I pull into a friend's driveway for a potluck dinner, eager to meet a Canadian family he has told me about. My six-month legal stay in the U.S. as a Canadian visitor expires next month, and I feel strongly that I am to remain in the country. But how?

Maybe the Hunters, who recently moved here from British Columbia, will tell me.

Or not…

"I'm a dual citizen," Calen Hunter explains.

So much for immigration advice.

"Your name," I say. "It's unusual."

"It's my spiritual name."

He has my attention. I pepper him with questions: How did he choose it? Did he change it legally? What did his family think? How did he feel giving up his birth name? Twenty minutes later, we're finished.

So is Mark David Gerson.

When I walk out of the house and into the world a few hours later, it's as Akhneton Yoseyva.

Fear of judgment has always hung heavily on me. That's what kept me creatively blocked for so many years. That's what held me back from acknowledging my sexual orientation. That's what initially prevented me from owning the name Akhneton, from owning my authenticity.

Now, I must swallow my fears and reintroduce myself to the world. While it is easier to do in a town where taking on an unusual name is almost a rite of passage, I'm anxious. Yet within days, most everyone has forgotten that I was ever anyone other than Akhneton.

The Way of the Fool

The Fool knows he is a Fool and, with a Fool's wisdom, knows there is nothing else he needs to know…or to be.

The Fool wears no mask. The Fool adopts no pretense. The Fool is. She moves from one moment's existence to the next, fully herself in each new breath.

Thus, the Fool never judges his self-worth or compares himself to anyone or anything else. Nor does the Fool contemplate who, what or why she is, wonder why she is not someone or something else, or wish she could be someone or something else. Why would he when with every breath and every step he is nothing other than the fullness and Fool-ness of his authentic self?

The Fool is only and ever the perfect expression of her divine essence and soul's imperative, and she wears that with neither pride nor humility, for both pride and humility suggest the possibility of an alternative way of being.

For the Fool, there is none. There is simply the Way of the Fool.

Your Story

Meditation: The Mask

Have your Way of the Fool journal handy to record your thoughts, feelings and impressions. Allow at least 30 minutes for this experience, longer if you plan further explorations in your journal once you have completed the meditation.

Revisit "Getting Started" for more tips on how best to use this book's meditations, visualizations and meditative journeys.

Close your eyes. Let your hands fall to your lap if you're sitting, to your abdomen if you're lying down.

Breathe…deeply…in and out…in and out…in and out…letting your breath slow and deepen with each inhalation, with each exhalation.

As you breathe in and out, feel your jaw loosen…your shoulders drop…your whole body relax. Feel relaxation course through your body.

Feel it carried on your bloodstream. Feel your bloodstream as a river of calm, relaxation, love and empowerment. Of safety.

Know that at any time during this experience, if anything feels too dangerous, you can take a deep breath and open your eyes. All you have to do is suspend this meditative journey until you feel able to continue. You are safe. Always safe.

Continue to breathe, to breathe deeply into this

experience…into this journey into the heart of you. Focus on your breath, and as you inhale and exhale, I am going to ask you a series of questions. Either answer them in your mind within this meditative experience, or pause the meditation while you open your eyes and journal your answers in your Way of the Fool journal. Whichever works for you. There is no right or wrong way of doing it, just as there is no right or wrong answer to any of these questions.

So…my questions…

- What in your life and/or creative life are you self-conscious about? Are you most self-conscious about?

- What about yourself or your creativity do you fear? Do you refuse to experience or express out in the world?

Don't think too hard about this. Don't think at all. Simply let a few responses bubble up into your conscious awareness — without judgment and without censorship. Allow yourself to open. Allow yourself to be surprised.

Are you surprised?

Now, go deeper. Look into more places in your life and creative life where you are self-conscious. Peer into the dark closets of your reluctance, the dust-filled attics of your concealment, the clammy cellars of your fear.

- Where are you embarrassed? Ashamed?

- Where do you feel inadequate?

- Where are you afraid of being judged?

- Where are you holding yourself back?

- Where are you hiding?

- Where are you not willing to risk being seen?

Each of these places is a mask you wear out into the

world. Perhaps it's a mask you also wear in front of the mirror. Regardless, it is a mask. And like all masks, it separates you from the world…and from yourself.

I'd like you focus on one of those masks right now. Only one. Any one. Can you get a sense of what it looks like? You might not experience this visually, and that's okay. There is no right or wrong way to experience any part of this meditation.

Whether or not you can see the mask, what does it feel like? What does it feel like on your face? What does it feel like in your heart? More importantly, perhaps, what is that mask holding you back from feeling?

More important still: What is this mask holding you back from experiencing? From expressing? From creating? From being? From becoming?

Journal your answers if that feels right. Or let them bubble to the surface of your conscious mind. Either way, sit with them for a few minutes. Let them sit with you.

Do you know why you created that mask? Do you have a story that explains it? That justifies it? Of course, you do. We all have good and powerful reasons for the masks we wear. Or, more accurately, we *had* good reasons for creating those masks…once upon a time.

But that time is not this time. That time was then, when we needed their protection. This time is now, when we are stronger, braver and more aware than ever that our masks are not ours alone. They are everyone's. And because they are everyone's, they not only hold us back, they hold everyone back.

So, whatever your reason for donning that mask, however long ago you slipped it on, that reason no longer exists, at least not in the same way it did in that "once upon a time." Can you acknowledge that? And in acknowledging that, can you also acknowledge that that mask no longer serves you in the ways it was originally designed? And in acknowledging that, can you also acknowledge that it is holding back your creativity — holding *you* back — in some way? Some significant way?

And from that acknowledgment, can you consider lifting that mask from your face? Can you accept that it's okay to show your face, that it's okay to be yourself? To be yourself first to yourself? Can you accept that it's okay to come out of hiding? To let yourself be seen? To let yourself be vulnerable?

Take a deep breath. As deep as you can. Breathe in all the strength of the universe. Breathe in all the courage of the universe. Breathe in all the love of the universe.

Now, touch your hand to your face. To the mask. And as you do and as you breathe, fully and deeply, let the mask dissolve at your touch. Let it dissolve and reveal the beauty and light that you are. Let it reveal the divine perfection that you are. Let it reveal the humanity that you are.

Be with that unmasked face for a few moments. How does it feel? It's okay to feel scared if you do. It's natural to feel scared, to feel raw, to feel vulnerable. All that means is that you're feeling human. That's because feeling, whatever it is you feel, is what it means to be human.

It's also natural to feel lighter, freer, more authentic and more open to possibility and to the fullest expression of your potential — in your creativity and in your life.

Feel whatever you feel. Breathe into that feeling. Be okay with that feeling. Sit with that feeling for a few moments. Take some time to let that feeling evolve.

If this is not your first experience with this meditation and you feel able to dissolve another mask, go ahead and do it. If this is your first experience, be gentle with yourself. Give yourself time to fully integrate and embody what it feels like to have let go this one mask. You can always return tomorrow or next week to remove another.

Regardless, take all the time you now need to remain in this meditative space before becoming once more fully aware of your breath, your physical body and your surroundings as a prelude to stepping back into your everyday life, now lighter, freer and more authentically you.

Try This

If you haven't already, write about your experiences in your Way of the Fool journal.

And Try This

Express your experiences in another creative medium. Find a creative way to do it in your usual medium, but also stretch yourself by playing in a different one. You could, for example, draw your mask or do a self-portrait — first, with the mask and now, having shed it. You could film or photograph your face or full body, as it might have been when you had your mask in place and now, having been freed from it. Improvise what it felt like with the mask and, now, without — with your voice, with your hands, with your body or with a musical instrument. Find the way that works for you, and have fun with this expression of your authenticity.

Ask Yourself These Questions

Explore these questions in your Way of the Fool journal. Don't think about the answers, and don't feel as though you must answer each question individually if that doesn't feel right. It's okay to find your own way.

Let all your answers (or whatever single answer these

questions trigger) emerge freely and honestly, writing them on the Muse Stream in a free-flowing, stream-of-consciousness way where appropriate.

Part I

- Where in my creative work am I refusing to reveal myself to the world?
- Where in my creative work am I refusing to reveal myself to me?
- Where in my creative work am I holding myself back from creating from places of powerful emotion, especially those emotions I tend to avoid?
- Where in my creative work am I holding myself back from walking the earth naked, clothed only in my truth?
- Where in my creative work am I refusing to be vulnerable and authentic?
- How else am I censoring myself in my creative work?

Part II

- Where am I letting myself shine through the words of my creative work for myself and for others?
- What am I discovering about myself as I create?
- What else would my creative work reveal to me about me if I let it?
- How can I start on a path to greater vulnerability and authenticity? What one step can I take today?

Creating on the Muse Stream

Revisit "Creating on the Muse Stream" from Step #1, and repeat the exercise.

When You're Finished…

Now that you have removed at least one of the masks holding you back from your fullest creative expression, how was this session different from others you have experienced? In process? In content? In emotional response? In resistance? Take a few minutes and note those differences, along with how the experience made you feel, in your Way of the Fool journal.

The Way of the Authentic Fool

Melissa Bernstein had it all. Melissa & Doug, the wildly popular toy company she'd cofounded in 1988, had sold billions of dollars of low-tech kids' products, all of which she had personally designed, and the company was worth $500 million. Bernstein also had a fairy tale family life, complete with a doting husband, six terrific kids and an enviably affluent lifestyle.

Yet things weren't what they seemed.

"From my earliest recollections," Bernstein told CBS in 2021, "I felt like I didn't belong here on earth, and that something was profoundly wrong deep within my being." The result, she says, was an "existential depression" that she was desperate to hide from the world. Who would want to see the dark, despairing woman she really was when she didn't want to see it herself?

To dull her "invisible ache," Bernstein filled every waking hour with activity. And to mask "the reality of who I was," she presented herself as living a perfect life.

The facade couldn't last.

One morning in her forties, she woke up and *woke up*. Her spiritual suffocation had become unbearable. "I'm living a lie," she realized. "This isn't who I am."

It was in that moment of surrender that Bernstein's journey to authenticity and self-acceptance began.

The result was a memoir, *Lifelines: An Inspirational Journey from Profound Darkness to Radiant Light*, and a website, www.lifelines.com. More than a website, Lifelines is an app, a podcast series, a video series, talks and events — all of it free.

As she shared her story, authentically and vulnerably, Bernstein experienced something extraordinary. Instead of the rejection and judgment she'd feared since childhood, she found empathy and connection.

"For most of my life," Bernstein says, "I believed I had to hide the parts of me that were flawed in order to be loved. Now I know that love only reaches us when we let ourselves be fully seen."

My Story: Coda I

Five and a half months after adopting my new name, I leaned into the clerk's counter at the county courthouse in Camp Verde, Arizona. Next to me stood Kentia Kazantzis, my wife-to-be. We were applying for a marriage license.

When the clerk printed Mark David Gerson, my legal name, on the form, Kentia blanched. She shifted her gaze from the license to me to the clerk and back to the license.

Then she pointed a finger at the offending line. "Can you add something to that?" she asked the clerk. "Like a nickname?"

"Like Bubba?" the clerk asked, in all solemnity.

"No," Kentia and I exclaimed in unison.

Once again, Kentia (who had met me as Akhneton Yoseyva, not as Mark David Gerson) looked from the name on the form to me and back.

"I'm not marrying Mark David Gerson," she declared with grim finality. "I'm marrying Akhneton Yoseyva."

I swallowed hard and turned to the clerk. I'd never planned to make my name change official. Calen hadn't… "If I wanted to change my name legally," I asked haltingly, "what would I have to do?"

The clerk explained the procedure, which in pre-9/11 Arizona was liberal enough that even a Canadian who was not yet a permanent resident could do it.

She handed me the necessary forms.

I could do it, but would I?

"I need to think about this," I pleaded.

"Here's what I can do," the clerk offered. "I'll make the license out in your birth name. If you decide to change it, come back with your papers and I'll issue you a new one at no charge."

Two days later, I was back at the same counter, this time with completed, notarized name-change forms. Two weeks later, Mark David Gerson legally ceased to exist. I was Akhneton Yoseyva, in law.

A few years later in Hawaii, another legal procedure would transform Akhneton into Aq'naton, but that's another story.

My Story: Coda II

I would remain Aq'naton until January 2005, two months after our marriage ended. Having sold our household goods and split the proceeds with my ex, I was back on the road.

On this day, I was driving along California's Pacific Coast Highway when, suddenly, the name "Aq'naton" no longer felt like it fit. I swerved into the next pullout and, shaken, stared at the ocean, steel-gray on this overcast day. If I wasn't Aq'naton, who was I? Was I Mark again? David? Neither felt right.

Over the next days, I called myself, variously, Mark, David and Aq'naton. None seemed to express my authentic self. Perhaps, I thought sinkingly, nothing can.

"What about 'Mark David,'" a friend suggested over lunch a week later in Sedona.

"Mark David? Mark David." I repeated it a few times. It felt odd, this unusual compound name that stumbled awkwardly off my tongue. "I don't know…" I pronounced it a few times more, each repetition slightly less clumsy. "Mark David. Mark David. Maybe…"

By the time I left the restaurant, there was no "maybe" about it. "Mark David" not only fit, it felt, well, authentic.

A few days later, I drove to the Camp Verde courthouse, back to the scene of that first legal name change. In Arizona at the time, name-changes did not require legal notices in a newspaper. They involved a summary hearing before a judge. The first time, my court appearance took place a few weeks after I handed in the paperwork in a session filled with uncontested divorces and other quick-gavel decisions. This time, I was only passing through Sedona, with no plans to stay beyond the next few days.

"I'll be traveling," I told the clerk when she offered possible court dates weeks out. "Are there no other options?"

"Hang on a sec," she said, and disappeared into a back room. Five minutes later, she reemerged. "Can you be back here in two hours?"

I nodded.

She grinned. "I found a judge who will give you a private hearing."

Three hours later, I was in Division Six of the Superior Court of Arizona.

"Why are you changing your name?" the judge asked.

I told him Aq'naton had been a pen name and that I now wanted all my affairs back in my birth name. It was the simplest piece of a larger truth.

He scribbled something onto his pad. "Are you changing your name to avoid debts or to hide from creditors?"

"No, sir."

He scribbled something else, signed the name-change order and passed it to the clerk. She stamped it.

It was 11:11 on January 27, 2005. Six years and eight months to the day after Akhneton Yoseyva had been legally created in this same building, he ceased to exist. Mark David Gerson had been reborn.

Declaration

I, *your name*, commit to creating from a place of open-heartedness, vulnerability and authenticity, courageously refusing to censor or second-guess the soul expressions that yearn to reveal themselves — to myself and to the world. And so it is.

Step #5. Dive into the Mystery

It is best not to know too much too soon. It is best to know only that the story continues and to follow where it takes you.
THE MOONQUEST, THE LEGEND OF Q'NTANA, BOOK 1

You carry an ocean of creation within you,
an infinite wellspring of ideas, emotions and exploits
that can sometimes surface to conscious awareness
only in the expression of them.

Like the mightiest of the earth's seas,
your ocean of creation is a place of magic and mystery,
a place of danger and delight...
a medley of the known and the unexplored,
a blend of the murky and the magnificent.

You dive into that ocean when
you embark on any creative expression.
And like all the great explorers
who have preceded you,
you may think you know
what you will find on your odyssey.

Even as you will surely encounter the expected,

this journey into your ocean of creation
will more often astound you as it reveals
treasures you never realized were there.

It will also occasionally alarm you as it reveals
thoughts and beliefs long ago buried.

Don't let your ocean's uncharted depths
frighten you into abandoning the adventure.

Dive in.
Dive into the magic.
Dive into the mystery.

My Story

WHEN DOROTHY GALE opens her eyes to discover that she and Toto aren't in Kansas anymore, her sole aim in setting off on the Yellow Brick Road is to get to the Emerald City, not to stay but to entreat the Wizard of Oz to use his magic to return her home. My goal when a metaphorical tornado blew me out of my Sedona condo in early 2023 was somewhat different: to find a new home *in* the Emerald City.

At least that was what I assumed. After all, why would I leave Sedona…only to return?

Like Dorothy, I couldn't know what gifts and hazards might lie along the Yellow Brick Road, nor could I know how long the journey to my Emerald City would take. Also like Dorothy, I couldn't know what would await me there. I couldn't even be certain that my conception of the Emerald City would turn out to be an accurate one. One thing I did know was that, wizard or no wizard, it would take some pretty potent magic to get me there and keep me there, wherever "there" turned out to be.

It had been an earlier Yellow Brick Road that dropped me in Sedona in August 2019, three months after a financial meltdown booted me out of Portland, an odyssey I chronicle in *Pilgrimage: A Fool's Journey.*

Now, a new financial crisis was pushing me out of Sedona: My condo's owner was returning from Italy to reoccupy the unit, and I lacked the wherewithal to rent a replacement in a pricey tourist town overrun by Airbnbs.

And because I'd never recovered from a covid-related financial crisis that had shuttered my workshop venue and, ultimately, stripped me of most of my coaching clients, I didn't see how I could afford reasonable housing costs anywhere.

That was the surface reason I set out on my Yellow Brick Road. Yet there were deeper ones. Heart reasons. Soul reasons. Reasons that only a Fool would understand and act on.

All my condo's owner did was accelerate the inevitable and set in motion a journey much different than the one I had anticipated…or would (consciously) have preferred.

Instead of propelling me onto the express lane to what I assumed to be my Emerald City, it pushed me onto nearly eighty thousand meandering Yellow Brick miles that carried me through fifteen states (most, multiple times), with none of the resources any prudent person would have had in place before leaving.

"If I were to choose an archetype to describe my life's journey," I write in my *Acts of Surrender* memoir, "it would be the Fool, a tarot character often pictured stepping off a cliff into the unknown."

I shouldn't have been surprised, then, that I was being asked to dive into another mystery, in faith. That's what the Fool does…again and again and again. Yet I was surprised, and stressed.

Perhaps had I reread my own words, I might have viewed my imminent journey through a different lens. Here's how I put in the opening to Step #12½ ("Fly Free") in *The Way of the Fool*.

"The Way of the Fool is a voyage of faith. There are no paved roads, worn paths or marked trails. There are only the roads, paths and trails that you yourself blaze. There are no predetermined routes or fixed GPS coordinates.

There is only the direction that calls you in this moment... and now in this one.

"Yes, it can seem random. But the heart's journey is never random. Yes, it can seem erratic. But the soul's journey is never erratic."

Therein lies one fundamental difference between Dorothy's road and mine. Hers was laid with visible cobblestones. All she needed to do, as directed by her Munchkin friends, was to "follow the Yellow Brick Road." Yes, it took courage, heart and brains to do so. Yet at least she could see the physical path ahead.

My Yellow Brick Road was an invisible one, cloaked in mystery. For all the asphalt highways I traveled, the true journeying was along the inner highways of my soul. And the only way I could know where to go, where to pause, where to start up again and where, in the end, to stop was to rely not on my car's GPS but on my own, a *God* Positioning System powered by my heart, my intuition and my inner knowingness. By the Way of the Fool.

That, too, took courage, heart and brains. And faith. Lots of faith. Faith that in surrendering to the voice of my heart and trusting it to guide me along this invisible Yellow Brick Road, I would find my way, safely, to whichever "wherever" was waiting for me at my journey's end.

My faith was not absolute, nor was it unshakable. That's the thing about faith. It never stops challenging you to believe in its absolute power. It certainly challenged me, just about every day. It also proved itself, just about every day.

In the end, as it always does, it carried me along the roads I needed to travel and through the experiences I needed to live, dropping me not where I expected to be and not where I thought I wanted to be. Rather, it dropped me where the wisdom of the Fool determined I needed to be, at the end of one mystery and the beginning of another.

The Way of the Fool

The Fool prepares neither lists nor plans. She drafts no itineraries. He sketches no outlines. She shuns schedules, rejects routine.

Of what value are maps, however roughly drawn, when every journey can only be a new one? What purpose the most meticulously charted course when even the same road cannot be traveled twice in the same manner?

For the Fool, each step, however taken and in whichever direction, carries him deeper into the mystery. And each mystery, whatever the experience and wherever it conveys her, carries her deeper into Fool-ish mastery.

When you dive into the unknown and relish the unknowable, you walk the Way of the Fool.

Your Story

Exploration • The Seeds of Creation

It wasn't until I was forty and living in the fertile farm country of Nova Scotia's Annapolis Valley that I experienced my first real garden. Frankly, it wasn't much of a garden; more a postage-stamp vegetable patch. Yet, tiny as it was, it was abundant with carrots, cucumbers, spinach, beans, tomatoes...and lettuce.

I remember feeling like Jack of *Jack and the Beanstalk* as I ripped open that first packet of lettuce seeds and held those magic specks in my palm before sprinkling them into the soil I had prepared.

With a plant, the evidence of creation is always visible. But when you sow from seed, you operate in the realm of mystery...the realm of faith. Once that seed is covered over, all you can do is trust, water and wait.

My miracle wasn't as dramatic as Jack's. It was a pale green frond, delicate against the rusty soil. Yet that dainty lettuce leaf was as magical to me as any giant beanstalk.

Much of the magic resided in the effortlessness of the enterprise. My sole task had been to drop the seeds into the ground, trust the dark mystery of Mother Earth, and wait. When the time was right for both of us, that lettuce leaf pushed through the moist earth and cried out, "Here I am!"

Creative expression can be just as effortless. Buried in the dark mystery of our unconscious lie the seeds of creation. They, like my lettuce seeds, dwell in a universe beyond our visual, tactile, mind-centered world. Like my lettuce leaf, they emerge in their time, when the season is right, when the moment is ripe.

You believe your inner place is devoid of ideas? Trust in the darkness and silence of the earth. Trust in the fertility of your creative process. Trust in the seeds that lie dormant beneath the surface. Trust that what needs to emerge will emerge when you create the conditions for that emergence, when you allow yourself the same space and silence you allow your seeds. Trust in the seasons of your creativity, and the fruits of that creativity will break through.

Today, take time to nurture the seeds now germinating in the dark earth of your being. Sit in the silence without poking and prodding, without questioning and analyzing. Be the seed you are and let the green shoots of your new growth develop and mature — into your awareness and into form.

Try This

Sometimes we're so busy doing, we never stop to be, to listen, to wait. Before you launch into creation today, give yourself 5, 10 or 20 minutes of nothingness…of silence…of emptiness. Sit in that silence as a seed sits in the soil. Breathe in the silence and breathe out your thoughts. Be in the stillness…breathe in the stillness…listen…and wait.

When you're ready to ease into creation, notice any differences in how you feel. Are you more, or less, anxious, fearful, ready? When you begin, notice any differences in what you're creating, how you're creating…the quality of the experience…the quantity of the output.

After Creation

What did the silence feel like, produce, open you to? Write

about that in your Way of the Fool journal, on the Muse Stream, using any or all these key phrases:

- In the silence, I…
- Through the silence, I…
- The silence guides me to…
- Because of the silence, I hear the still, small voice of my Muse. It…

Meditation: Genesis

Have your Way of the Fool journal handy to record your thoughts, feelings and impressions. Allow at least 15 minutes for this experience. Allow additional time after the meditation if you plan further explorations — in your journal or through creative expression.

Revisit "Getting Started" for more tips on how best to use this book's meditations, visualizations and meditative journeys.

Close your eyes and get comfortable. Allow your body to relax. Breathe in as deeply as you can and let it go. And again. And again.

Breathe in calm…peace…centeredness.

Breathe out fear…doubt…judgment. Breathe in to your creative voice…your creative essence…your creative spirit.

Breathe out anything and everything that is not in alignment with that.

Now, let your shoulders drop and feel all stress and all strain drain from them and from your neck, where we carry so much heaviness, so much anxiety. And from your shoulders, where we carry all our responsibilities, all our obligations…all our shoulds.

Feel the tension around your eyes lighten. Too often, we scrunch our eyes and foreheads, trying to focus, trying to see…to see everything.

For right now, you don't have to try to see everything…to try to see anything. You don't have to try to do anything…to be anything.

Simply let yourself be as you are. Now. Right now.

And from that place of being, allow. Allow yourself to travel on these words and into the realm of inner vision, *your* inner vision…to the realm to which these words carry you…to which your Muse and your creative spirit carry you. To do more than allow. To surrender, to whatever and wherever your inner vision, your Muse, your creative spirit, your creative source, carries you.

Instead of inviting you to envision or imagine a place, person or thing, which I often do in these meditations and visualizations, I am going to invite you to imagine *nothing*.

Total emptiness.

A black, blank void. A blank slate, if you will.

Take yourself back in time to the moments before the Big Bang, when nothingness was all there was. Or take yourself back to the earliest moments of that first day of Creation where, as Genesis puts it, "the earth was formless, and empty, darkness was over the surface of the deep."

Formless. Empty. Darkness. Nothingness.

A black, blank void.

I say "time" and "moments before." But there isn't time and there aren't moments. There aren't even breaths. Even the word "nothing" suggests an absence…the absence of some thing. There is no some-thing and never has been.

This is perfect oblivion. A black, blank void.

Breathe into that, that emptiness, that void. Breathe into it and be okay with it. There is nothing to fear in that emptiness, no reason to feel uneasy or overwhelmed by the vastness of the void, no reason to feel hopeless in the face of that vacant formlessness.

On the contrary, there is every reason to feel hopeful.

That's because this emptiness, this vacuum, is not a permanent state, cannot be a permanent state. It's a starting point. A beginning.

A genesis.

For it is from the black, blank void, from the empty darkness, that all creation emerges — for me, for you, for every creative artist in every medium. It has been true throughout history, back to that first creative artist, the God of Genesis. And it's true today…just as it will be tomorrow and for every other tomorrow all the way into the timelessness of infinite time.

So breathe into that empty darkness. Breathe into it and surrender into it. One breath. Another breath.

And another.

Now, let your next breath be the Big Bang breath of physics…the "let there be light" breath of Genesis…the breath that ignites the spark of creation. *Your* creation.

Take that next breath.

See that spark. Feel that spark.

With your next breath, let that spark kindle a flame. And feel that. The heat of it. The passion of it.

And with your next breath, let that flame explode into a brilliant, fiery light, the light that illuminates this new universe that is the creation of your heart…the gift of your Muse, of your creative spirit.

What do you see or sense in this universe? Engage all your physical senses to immerse yourself in it.

What do you see? It may be clear. People. Places. Objects. Shapes. Colors. Cloud formations. Birds. Animals. Or it may be more vague, indefinite. Whatever it is is perfect. Don't judge. Don't second-guess. Don't censor. Allow. Let it be whatever it is. And let it evolve into something else, if that's what it needs to do, chooses to do.

So what do you see?

And touch. What can you touch? Or what can you imagine touching if there's nothing you can reach out and touch? What can you touch? Could you touch?

And smell. What can you smell? Or what can you imagine smelling if there's no scent associated with this universe? What can you smell? Could you smell?

And taste. What can you taste? Or what can you imagine tasting? Or what would what's in your universe taste like if it had a taste? What can you taste? Could you taste?

Finally, sound. What can you hear? What kinds of sounds can you hear? It could be clear and identifiable, or it could be indistinct. It could be music. It could be birdsong or animal sounds. It could be the wind whispering through the trees. It could be voices.

It could be a message — a direct one or an indirect one, one you intuit. What can you hear?

Don't forget your nonphysical senses. Engage those too. What is the spirit of this universe? Its essence? Its quintessence? Its soul?

Its story. What is its story?

In a few moments, I am going to ask you to open your eyes and translate this universe, this vision of your heart, this vision of your Muse into story…in the broadest sense of the notion of "story." In other words, it doesn't have to be a written story. It can be a story expressed in any creative medium…or in more than one creative medium.

First, though, I'd like you to spend a few more breaths with this universe. Explore it in any additional ways that will carry you deeper into it…that will further illuminate it…that will expand your sense of it, your feel of it, your vision of it. Your story of it.

Now, holding that fire, that universe, that vision, in your consciousness, slowly return your awareness to your breath…to your body…to whatever you're sitting on or lying on…to your surroundings.

When you're ready, gently open your eyes and free your spark of creation, the flame of your passion and the fire of your vision to illuminate your way as you bring your universe into form. So pick up the tools of your creativity and create on the Muse Stream — freely and without judgment, without second-guessing and without self-censorship.

Create what is uniquely yours to create, what only you can create. Immerse yourself in the experience of genesis, taking all the time you need to give life and substance to this universe, the universe of your creation.

When You're Finished…

How was this creative session different from others you have experienced? In process? In content? In emotional response? In resistance? Take a few minutes and note those differences, along with how the experience made you feel, in your Way of the Fool journal.

The Way of the Murderous Fool

When author J.A. Jance starts a new novel in her four mystery series, she knows no more than will her readers when they turn to the first page of the published book. That's because Jance not only writes mystery, she writes *into* the mystery, never planning, plotting or outlining her stories. She starts with a dead body and trusts the voice of her Muse to tell her whodunit and how.

"I have to sort of step out with faith," she said to me in a 2013 interview, "that if I can write the first sentence of the book, I can eventually get to the end of it."

That act of faith has never failed her…or her legions of fans. At eighty-one, Jance has produced more than eighty books, many of which have topped the *New York Times* bestseller list. And she's still going.

My Story: Coda

In the end, like Dorothy's, my Yellow Brick Road carried me home — not back to where I'd begun, but also not to the Emerald City I'd expected. Instead, as it has done so often in the past, it carried me to the home of my heart's desire… one my conscious mind could never have imagined. It also carried me to the start of a whole new journey, one that is still unfolding. But that's a story for another book… because in my life there is always another book.

Declaration

I, *your name*, dive into the unknown, relish the unknowable and surrender to the mystery that lies at the heart of all creation. And so it is.

Step #6. Create in the Moment

As always, I will undertake to follow my heart, moment-to-moment and day-by-day, in trust that I will continue to be taken care of...through this journey and beyond.
Pilgrimage: A Fool's Journey

surrender
to the boundless
All
that you are

immeasurable
unquantifiable
eternal

each moment a lifetime
repeating and unrepeatable

an Omnipresence that spirals inexorably
into infinity

My Story

PENETANGUISHENE (Penetang to locals) is a small community at the southeastern tip of Georgian Bay, a massive Lake Huron inlet that's nearly as large as all of Lake Ontario. It became my home in October 1997, a move I'd planned as an open-ended retreat that would free me to work on *The MoonQuest*.

That was the plan.

It wasn't the result.

In the end, my five months in Penetang turned out to be a time of profound emotional healing, and the resulting book was something else altogether: a memoir of my sojourn there, titled *Dialogues with the Divine: Encounters with My Wisest Self.*

When I arrived on the afternoon of my forty-second birthday, fall was already drawing to a close this far north. And as the season stripped the trees of their gold and crimson leaves, it stripped me too — leaving me as bare and vulnerable as the oaks, birches and maples that clambered up the treed slopes behind my new home.

My morning routine in those early days was to take my cocker spaniel, Roxy, for a long walk in those woods before breakfast. Then I would return to my two-room granny flat to eat before settling into my day.

Even bare of leaves, the trees created a womb-like oasis for me after ten months in the relentless noise and bustle of Toronto. Yet for all the sylvan peace of those fall mornings,

I couldn't still my mind enough to enjoy my surroundings. Instead, I would spend my forty-five minutes outdoors focusing not on the scenery but on worry. What I would eat when I got back? How would I spend my day? Why had I been pulled out of Toronto when I wasn't yet working on *The MoonQuest*?

It took a few weeks, but once I realized how my mind was hijacking what should have been a meditative, now-moment experience, I developed an exercise to keep me present. Each time I noticed my mind wandering back to my fridge and my day and anything beyond my woodland refuge, I turned my attention to my senses. What was I hearing? What was I seeing? What was I smelling?

"I hear the birds," I would say out loud. "I see the grain on the tree trunk. I smell the decay of rotting leaves." Or I would take off my glasses and pay attention only to what I could see without them, and speak that aloud.

Some days, the exercise immediately banished my out-of-the-moment anxiety. Other days, I had to continue my enforced mantra-mindfulness until I got home.

It worked. By the time I left Penetang the following spring, my early mornings had evolved into joyfully meditative preludes to days that had, themselves, grown easier.

The Way of the Fool

The Fool never projects himself forward to tomorrow or to the tomorrow after that or the tomorrow after that. Why leap ahead to a virtual moment that may never come to pass? Nor does the Fool dwell on yesterday or on previous or long ago yesterdays. Why revisit that which can be neither amended nor altered?

Just as the Fool cannot reexperience a breath already breathed, she cannot breathe one yet to born. The Fool lives and creates within each inhalation and each exhalation. He knows only this breath and moment…and now this breath and moment…and now this one.

It is no accident that the word "present" simultaneously suggests "existence," "now-time" and "gift." In effect, our presence exists only in the gift of the moment. When we refuse that gift by stepping out of the moment, we also step out of our presence and, in a sense, dilute our very existence.

Each time we worry about our fate or the fate of our creative expression, we remove ourselves from the present moment — a moment during which the cause of our anxiety is rarely an immediate threat or concern.

Each time we worry about anything, we project ourselves forward into a future we are desperate to control. Whether that future is moments, days, weeks, months or decades away, it is unlikely to show up as we expect it to. Regardless, we cannot control it.

Each time we censor our words, thoughts, actions or creations for fear of being attacked, condemned or censured, we remove ourselves from the present moment — a moment of truth sacrificed on the altar of potential consequences.

Each time we censor our words, thoughts, actions or creations, we deny our presence by denying our heart its voice and our soul its song.

Each time we judge or second-guess ourselves or our creative expression, we remove ourselves from the present moment — a moment in which whatever has triggered our judgment is no longer present.

Each time we judge or second-guess ourselves or our creations, we step back in time, to a moment in a past that not only no longer exists but that can never again be present.

The Way of the Fool is a breath-by-breath, moment-by-moment journey that neither looks back in judgment nor forward in anxiety. Nor does it attach itself to particular outcomes.

The Fool learns from the past, but not from a place of recrimination. The Fool plans and takes action toward the future, though not from a place of fear. The Fool has goals and objectives, but no expectations. Rather, the Fool deals identically with past, present and future: with heartful discernment and in a centered groundedness that is always anchored in the now.

When you walk the Way of the Fool, you live and create from the truth of this moment, this feeling, this breath, this creative act. Then you move on to the next moment, to live and create from its truth, its presence, its gift.

Your Story

Exploration • One Step at a Time

There's a scene in *The MoonQuest* where Toshar, the main character, steps onto a translucent road, his sole route back to earth from a celestial plateau high above the suns (there are two suns in the world of the book).

"I quickly learned," Toshar recounts in the story, "to train my eyes to look no more than a few paces ahead. At that distance, a faint, silvery glow marked out my path. It was almost opaque. Yet if I looked back or farther ahead, I saw no sign of road. No sign of anything." In Toshar's world, as in yours and mine, past and future have no substance.

Only the present moment exists...the present moment and the present moment of creation.

Don't look back and don't worry forward. As you create, whatever it is you are creating, stay in the moment of creation — with the word of the moment, the brushstroke of the moment, whatever this moment's creative action is for you.

That's the same journey I traveled in writing *The MoonQuest*, a book whose story I knew nothing about except as I wrote it. (See Step #7, "My Story: Coda I.") The novelist E.L. Doctorow has likened writing to driving at night in the fog. "You can only see as far as your headlights," he wrote, "but you can make the whole trip that way." You can make the whole trip that way whatever you are creating.

Some days, Doctorow's headlights will illuminate only the next step; some days, they will reveal the whole staircase. It doesn't matter which, because as we move forward — creating in the moment, moment-by-moment — whatever we next need to see or know will always reveal itself…if we are open to it. If we have our eyes on the road and our headlights on, if we are prepared to trust in the unknown that lies just beyond the reach of our vision, that unknown will become illuminated, known and manifest.

Try This

In whatever you're creating today, notice all the times your mind edges (or leaps) ahead of the immediate task at hand. Be aware as that controlling part of yourself reaches forward to find out what's coming next, where you're headed, how it will be when you're done. Notice when this happens, but don't judge or punish yourself. Instead, return your focus to the present moment. Return to it gently, lovingly, reassuringly. Then continue creating, in the moment, one moment at a time.

Try This Too

Take the experience I describe in "My Story" and make it your own. Go for a walk — in nature, around the block, along a busy street or anywhere that offers you some degree of sensory stimulation. As you walk, do your best to stay in the present moment, limiting your focus to your five senses and to what you are seeing, hearing, touching, smelling or tasting from breath to breath. If you find your mind wandering, make a point of acknowledging each stimulus, saying (aloud or silently), "I see/ smell/hear/touch/taste the…" Repeat the phrase as you walk, as often as necessary to keep focused on the now. By staying in the moment, we stay out of fear, worry and anxiety, prime causes of all blocks — in our lives as much as in our creativity.

Try This As Well

In your Way of the Fool journal, write on the Muse Stream using the key phrase "In this moment, I am…" as your kickoff. Don't think about what to write. Don't censor or second-guess what emerges. Free onto the page the words, thoughts and feelings that want to emerge and let them reveal to you where you truly are in this moment. After you have written for a few minutes, begin again using this key phrase: "In this moment, I create…"

And This…

Ask yourself this question in your Way of the Fool journal but don't think about the answer. Let it emerge freely and honestly on the Muse Stream: Where in my creative and life's journeys can I better stay anchored in the moment and more fully trust that the headlights illuminating my way will carry me safely to my unseen destination?

Meditation: In the Moment

This is an effective technique for pulling yourself back into the moment when you're feeling anxious. Use the following script, but also practice doing the meditation on your own, anywhere, to release anything distracting you from the present moment.

Have your Way of the Fool journal handy to record your thoughts, feelings and impressions. Allow at least 10 minutes for this experience, longer if you plan further explorations in your journal once you have completed the meditation.

Revisit "Getting Started" for more tips on how best to use this book's meditations, visualizations and meditative journeys.

Sit down — at your desk, in your favorite chair, in your favorite part of the garden, in your favorite park or on your favorite beach…wherever you feel comfortable, safe and inspired. Or lie down. Do whatever is easiest and most convenient.

Close your eyes, place your hands on your empty lap, or on your abdomen if you're lying down, and breathe…in and out slowly, as slowly as you can, for ten breaths.

Breathe more slowly and deeply with each breath, and feel yourself relax. Feel each inhalation connect you to your heart, to the moment and to your Muse.

Feel each exhalation flush all fear, doubt and anxiety from your emotional body…flush all worldly concerns from your mind.

As you continue to breathe in and out, let your breath dissolve all tightness from your physical body — from your neck and shoulders, from your chest and abdomen, from your mid- and lower back and from any other place where you cling to stress and tension.

Now, as your breath continues to slow and deepen, focus on your heart and breathe into it and into the only moment that exists: that place of the eternal now.

Picture yourself now in a park or on a beach, holding on to a bunch of brightly colored balloons, each with its own string. There's a slight breeze, and the balloons are bobbing around and bouncing into each other.

As you continue to relax and breathe, you may notice your mind straying from the present moment with a thought about the past or future. Perhaps you are replaying something from earlier in your day or from years back.

Or perhaps you are thinking ahead — to some aspect of a current or future creative project, to some past creative project…to a bill that needs paying…to an upcoming appointment…or to anything that is not of this moment, that is not of this breath.

Whatever your not-now thought, assign it to one of the balloons…to any balloon. Let an abbreviated version of your thought inscribe itself onto the surface of that balloon and, once it has, release the marked balloon and let it float up into the air.

Watch it rise higher and higher, and be aware of it growing smaller and smaller until, finally, it disappears into the distant sky. As it vanishes from view, let the thought you attached to it vanish as well.

Continue releasing your thought-balloons one-by-one until you are able to stay present in the moment with your breath. Then rest in the stillness of the eternal now until you feel complete with the experience.

When you do feel complete, slowly bring your awareness back to your physical body and to your surroundings.

Become conscious of your arms and legs, of your hands and feet, of your neck and shoulders. Move or shake them gently. Become aware again of your breath, of your heartbeat.

Notice any ambient sounds — in the room or beyond. What are you hearing? Sensing around you?

Now, become aware of whatever you are sitting or lying on. Let your fingers run over it and feel its texture, its temperature, its solidity, its hardness or softness. Its nowness.

When you're ready, let your eyes open and adjust to the light. Sit up if you're lying down. Connect once again with the physicality and energy of your surroundings.

Finally, and only when you feel it's time, allow yourself to reenter the world, whatever that means to you, from a place of the same moment-to-moment awareness you experienced in the meditation.

In the hours and days ahead, use this thought-balloon imagery to release anything pulling you from the present moment or away from the immediate requirements of the work you are creating.

Variation: If the balloon imagery doesn't work for you, or if you want to try an alternative, imagine yourself in a room holding a broom. Each time you feel pulled from the present moment, open the door and sweep that thought away.

Creating on the Muse Stream

Revisit "Creating on the Muse Stream" from Step #1, and repeat the exercise.

When You're Finished…

How was this creative session different from others you have experienced? In process? In content? In emotional response? In resistance? Take a few minutes and note those differences, along with how the experience made you feel, in your Way of the Fool journal.

The Way of Artistic Fool

What could be more in-the-moment than light? After all, both the quantity and quality of light in any given scene are constantly shifting. Depending on weather, climate and time of day, those shifts can be subtle, barely discernible to the naked eye, or they can be startlingly dramatic.

How do you capture that on canvas? Can you?

In 1892, Impressionist painter Claude Monet determined to try.

He rented a room directly across from Rouen Cathedral, the massive Gothic structure famous as the site of Joan of Arc's trial, and set up his easel. Although many artists had painted the cathedral's solid, intricate stonework over the years, none had attempted anything as audacious as the challenge Monet set for himself.

Monet was less interested in the building than in the way it received and reflected light, in the way light and shadow danced across its facade from moment to moment over the course of each day.

Instead of creating a single painting, Monet set up multiple canvases. As the sun moved and light changed, he moved his paints from one canvas to the next, doing his best to stay in sync with each moment.

By 1894 Monet had completed his Rouen series: thirty canvases that made the cathedral seem nearly as ephemeral as light itself. "Everything changes," he said, "even stone." Together, those paintings are a testament to the experience of presence, the only way to capture the truth of the moment.

Although Monet had hoped for all thirty to be displayed together, that never happened. Today, the Rouen Cathedral paintings are scattered among public and private collections around the world, including London's National Gallery, L.A.'s Getty Museum, Washington's National Gallery of Art, Moscow's Pushkin Museum and the Musée d'Orsay in Paris.

"One must know how to seize the moment of the landscape," Monet wrote, "for that moment will never return…"

My Story: Coda

I would like to be able to report that my Penetanguishene experience taught me to always stay present and to never let future-worry distract me from the now. I can't. Life doesn't work that way. Well, my life doesn't.

Instead, I use exercises like the one I developed during my time in Penetang, along with the balloon meditation I shared earlier in this section. And I continue to write and create on the Muse Stream, always a now-moment experience.

Declaration

I, *your name*, live and create in the eternal now. As the Fool that I am, I focus all my attention and intention on the creative act of the moment, knowing that, like my breath, the next will always come if I get out of my way and let creation create. And so it is.

Step #7. Trust Your Muse

Trust the voice of your Muse without judgment or censorship.
From Memory to Memoir: Writing the Stories of Your Life

Your Muse may trick you into discovering the unexpected, the undesired, the unwanted.

Your Muse may trick you into creating the unprecedented, the risky, the terrifying.

This is good.

Your Muse sees the higher perspective that you, sitting in the emptiness of the world before creation, cannot.

Curse and mutter if you must. Resist if you can.

Then embrace your Muse's boundless wisdom, surrender to its infinite vision, and journey wherever it sends you.

Trust your Muse. It is smarter than you are.
It understands your creative potential better than you ever will.
It will never let you down.

My Story

IT'S A FEBRUARY MORNING in 1992, early on my conscious journey of spiritual awakening. Desperate to distance myself from an endless loop of a nightmare, I force my eyes open into the predawn darkness of my Toronto bedroom. I get up, soaked in sweat, trying to shake off the dream. I can't. It haunts me through my shower…through my breakfast…and into my day. Finally, hoping I can force some sort of resolution, I take the nightmare into meditation.

In the dream, I'm clinging to the roof-ledge of a 1950s skyscraper, my feet dangling from the high-rise structure.

"Let go," a voice repeats, gently but insistently.

I peer down at the busy street hundreds of feet below and grip more tightly. How can I let get? If I do, I will die.

Yet the voice continues its urgings.

I can't do it. I don't do it. I don't let go.

My favorite place to meditate back then was the forest green wing chair in my living room. It was comfortable, its color was calming and its "wings" offered the illusion of a womb-like enclosure. It felt safe.

I needed the feeling of safety that morning as I shut my eyes, focused on my breath and let my mind carry me back into the scene of my nightmare.

Once again, I found myself clinging to the roof-ledge of that same building. Once again, that same voice pressed me to let go. Once again, I couldn't. Once again, I didn't. Instead, I held on, my fingers cramped and in pain.

When I opened my eyes some minutes later, nothing had been resolved.

I repeated the experience twice more in the next days, each time with identical results.

Determined to not let the nightmare defeat me a fourth time, I tried again a few days later.

I wish I could boast that I had grown more courageous. I wish I could boast that I had grown to trust the voice of my Muse-like intuitive self. I wish I could boast that I was now confident that I wouldn't plummet to my death were I to release my grip from an outmoded paradigm represented by a structure as old as I was.

If I did, it would be an empty boast. In truth, holding on had become so unbearable that I couldn't do it anymore.

"This can't be good," I muttered as, numbed, my fingers unclenched. In my meditative vision, I shut my eyes, fully expecting to slam into the pavement.

Barely a breath later, I opened them again. I wasn't tumbling. I wasn't hurtling. I was floating, feather-like… not into traffic, but into what I can only describe as the arms of God.

No, I didn't trust enough to let go willingly. Not that time. But I was more willing the next time and the time after that. And I learned not only that I could trust but that, when I did, the arms of God would always be waiting for me.

The Way of the Fool

When it comes to the Muse, or to any other expression of highest wisdom, the Fool does not grasp the concept of trust. For to accept that trust exists suggests that its opposite must also exist.

For the Fool, however, that opposite cannot exist, not in relation to any expression of highest wisdom and, thus, not in relation to the Muse, which, itself, is among the highest expressions of that highest wisdom.

The Fool does not trust, for the Fool does not need to trust.

The Fool knows.

The Fool knows that any guidance, direction, inspiration, intuition, sensation, impulse or prompt deriving from that infinite font of universal wisdom is faultless, flawless and unerringly sound — fully and Fool-ly. Therefore, whatever the guidance, direction, inspiration, intuition, sensation, impulse or prompt, the Fool follows it. She follows it unquestioningly, in the certainty that no better or higher course of action can exist in that moment.

When we live and act from that place of inner knowingness, in our art as elsewhere, we walk the Way of the Fool. In those all-too-human moments when we cannot touch that place of absolute certainty, we take a leap of faith. That, too, is the Way of the Fool.

Your Story

Exploration I • The Voice of Your Muse

The Muse speaks to us with that same "small, still voice" described in many spiritual traditions. There, we experience it as the breathings of God or Goddess, Source or Spirit, Universal or Infinite Mind, your higher or wisest self. Beyond spirituality, we might sense it as the whispers of intuition. In our creative lives, it's the voice of our most distinctive, most original artistic expression. When we listen for it, listen to it and trust it enough to surrender to it, it transports us into the magical, miracle-filled realm of the Creative Fool.

It can be difficult sometimes, even as creative artists, to bypass the skepticism and cynicism of our logical minds, trained as they are in trusting only what can be experienced with our five physical senses. But to borrow from Shakespeare and as every child knows, there are more things in heaven and earth than those five physical senses can discern. And when we reclaim our childhood sense of wonder and give ourselves permission to once again trust those non-physical sensings, we gain access to a world of creative possibility beyond any we can consciously imagine.

How do we get there? How do we attune our hearts and minds to that singular voice? How do we foster and nurture it?

The best way, of course, is to do your best to trust it and act on it whenever you sense an action to take, a decision to make or a course to chart — in your creativity, of course, but also in the rest of your life. The more you listen for it, the more you will hear it. And the more you heed it, the more wisdom and creative direction you will access.

Our Muse often speaks to us in metaphor: in signs and symbols, through visions and dreams, and in those meaningful coincidences Carl Jung called "synchronicities." It can also speak through physical sensations (goosebumps, a "truth shiver," a fluttering in the stomach) or through a hunch, an inner knowing or a gut feeling. Once again, the more aware we allow ourselves to be of these "messages" and the more we trust them, the more of them we will notice. And the more of them we notice and trust, the more we will train ourselves to bypass the logical, conventional, sensible, status quo cues that our minds prefer in favor of the unexpected, the unconventional, the unexplainable, the un-sensicle.

Each of the following explorations will help you awaken, access, experience and express some aspect of your Muse as it guides you along the Way of the Creative Fool.

Lose Your Mind and Come to Your Senses

Any activity that stops you from intellectualizing, analyzing or overthinking, that refocuses your attention from head to heart or that pulls your awareness back into the present moment opens a portal into an experience of your Muse. Try any or all of these…

- ***Creating on the Muse Stream:*** This is an effective way to get out of your head and explore your dormant creative gifts. Many exercises and explorations in *The Way of the Creative Fool*, including the Inner Dialogue exercise later in this section, call on you to create in that spontaneous, free-flowing way.

Need a Muse Stream refresher? Revisit "Your Muse and You" and the explorations in Step #1.

- ***Meditation, Guided Visualization and Guided Journeys:*** Any of this book's meditation scripts, including "Meet Your Muse" in the "Your Muse and You" section and the "Quick Centering Meditation" in Step #1, will put you in a receptive space, as will any meditative experience.

- ***Centering Physical Activity:*** Yoga, tai chi and qigong are among the disciplines that are at the same time physical and meditative. Running can often achieve similar results, as can a hike or a walk in nature.

- ***Tub Time:*** A relaxing soak in the bath or in a hot tub, especially with dim lighting and contemplative music, can help you get past what Buddhists call "monkey mind" and open up an unobstructed channel to the voice of your Muse.

- ***Passionate Pursuit:*** It's easy to enter into a Zen state of peace, presence, possibility and receptivity — into the "zone," as athletes typically describe it — when we immerse ourselves in a passionate pursuit, be it our usual creative medium or some other passion.

Signs, Symbols and Synchronicities

Signs can show up in various ways to help guide you in your creative life.

As you move through your day, pay close but not obsessive attention to your surroundings. Notice when odd things happen. Pay attention to people, places and objects that might carry symbolic significance, and be aware of coincidences that seem more meaningful than random. Do the same with your dreams. Log as many as you can in your Way of the Fool journal, daily if possible, even if you can't immediately interpret what you see and experience.

The more you acknowledge the possibility of deeper meaning, the more that potential will make itself known in your creativity and throughout your life…and the more clearly it will tend to express itself.

When it comes to interpreting what you see, sense and hear, let dictionaries of signs and symbols be your resource of last resort. Rely first on what individual symbols mean to you. Go with first thoughts, and don't second-guess or censor yourself. The Way of the Creative Fool is about trusting your intuition and your gut. So trust them.

The Music of Your Muse

If you're tuned in to it, music can also serve as the voice of your Muse. Listen for snatches of songs you happen to hear. A seemingly random lyric or song title might offer a signal, a hint or some information regarding a question you might have, a decision you might be struggling with, a direction you might be contemplating or some aspect of a current creative project or one you are considering. Some might also provide validation, confirmation or reassurance.

If you're like me, you might hear part of a song playing in your head while you're in that hypnagogic state between waking and sleep. That's another way your Muse can communicate with you.

Log these, too, in your Way of the Fool journal.

Listen to Your Body

Your body has an innate wisdom, and your Muse and intuition often express themselves through it — sometimes painfully obviously, sometimes more subtly. Pay attention to your physical reactions to people and situations, to good news and bad news, to choices you have made or are about to make. Be aware of uncomfortable or unusual sensations. The most common tend to occur on your skin, in your stomach or in your chest, or at the top of your forehead or the base of your skull. But they could show up anywhere and in any way.

When anything like that happens, explore it and your feelings toward it through creative expression or in your Way of the Fool journal.

Consult an Oracle

Whether you have a question you want answered or are open to whatever your Muse is ready to communicate, pick a card at random from a tarot or other oracle deck. Use a deck whose cards don't have basic meanings printed on them and, instead of looking up the card's meaning, let your Muse reveal its significance to you in that moment.

What's your first thought about it? About what it might represent for you right now?

Not sure? Don't analyze the card. Instead, gaze at it in a right-brain, overview sort of way. What leaps out at you? It could be something integral to the main image or something barely perceptible off in a corner. Whatever it is, focus your attention on it; again, not in a logical, analytical way. Focus on your emotions, your gut feelings, your physical sensations. How does the card as a whole or that first thing you noticed make you feel?

Nothing leaps out at you? Not a problem. What story are the images on the card telling you? Start telling the story — silently or in your Way of the Fool journal — and notice what you're focusing on, how the story is making you feel and any associations to your life or creativity that you are drawing from it.

If you are feeling challenged to get out of your logical mind, write your thoughts, impressions, stories and feelings on the Muse Stream.

Regardless of how you approach this, do your best to not censor or second-guess what you see, sense and feel, and don't worry if your interpretation bears no resemblance to the card's classic interpretation. When it comes to your intuition, there are no right or wrong answers.

- *Try using a tarot or oracle card to spark new ideas and creative projects. That's how "The MoonQuest" came to be, a story I share in "My Story: Coda I," below.*

Intuition by the Book

As with the oracle-card draw, either ask a question for which you would like an answer or be open to whatever your Muse is ready to communicate.

Pick up a book. It can be a book you're in the midst of reading, a favorite title or anything from your shelf or from a library or bookstore shelf. Open it to a random page and note the first word, phrase or sentence that catches your eye.

Does that word, phrase or sentence answer your immediate question or one you have been pondering? Does it offer some sort of clarity? Does it spark an idea for a creative project? It might do so in an obvious way, but it could as easily be mysterious and obtuse — at least to your logical mind.

If it's the former, your work is done...or nearly. All that remains is for you to honor your Muse by following whatever guidance it has sent you. If it's the latter, it might require some interpretation.

Try to avoid overanalyzing it. Rather, practice your intuitive skills by adapting some of the techniques you used in "Consult an Oracle." Or, as I suggest in "Consult an Oracle," let the word, phrase or sentence act as a prompt for some form of creative expression.

Regardless, explore the experience in your Way of the Fool journal.

Inner Dialogue

What I call "inner dialogue" is a powerful Muse Stream tool that allows you to communicate directly with your Muse (in truth, your unconscious mind) and get answers to questions or decisions you're struggling with.

It's a tool I have used often over the years, including during the period I describe in Step #6's "My Story." I collected the writings from that time into my book *Dialogues with the Divine*. I also used the technique for the encounters with *MoonQuest* characters I mention in Step #3.

Adapt the guidelines that follow in whatever way feels most relevant and appropriate to your situation. Remember, though, that the goal is to let go all control of the process and to trust your Muse, your intuition and your inner sensings, both in terms of how you approach the experience and how you view the results.

Settle into a physical, emotional and spiritual state of stillness. If you have a meditation practice, do what you normally do to get into a receptive space. If not, close your eyes and sit quietly, focusing on your breath to silence your mind. Use music, aromatherapy, crystals, yoga or ritual if you find any or all of these to be helpful. Alternatively, use the "Meet Your Muse" meditation in "Your Muse and You" to relax you and guide you through the experience.

Either start with a consciously posed question, feeling or comment or allow one addressed to you to bubble up into your awareness. Your dialogue can be with your inner critic, your fear or your inner child. It can be with a character if you're writing fiction, with the subject in your visual art or with a relevant tool, component or ingredient. It can be with your project as a whole or with a particular aspect of the project. It can be with your Muse or higher self. It can be with God, Spirit or Source.

Some days, it might start out as staticky mind noise. That's okay. Writing that nattering chatter will give it voice and, ultimately, silence it.

Whichever side of the conversation first bubbles up into your awareness, begin with that. Then let a response — yours or the "other side's" — emerge spontaneously on the Muse Stream. If you're posing a question, don't look for an answer. Don't think about an answer. *Let* the answer.

Whatever the tenor and content of your back-and-forth, don't force it. Free it to be whatever it needs to be... whatever you need it to be.

The key in both sides of your dialogue, as with any Muse Stream experience, is to write without stopping, censoring or second-guessing. Write for as long as you feel the need to, and then a little longer after that. The wisest words and deepest truths often emerge after we think we're done.

If, when you're finished, you doubt the value of what has emerged, don't read it right away. Instead, set your writing aside for at least an hour or until you are able to look at what you have written uncritically and without judgment. Then, read it with an open heart and an open mind to discover what inner wisdom you have uncovered.

- *Need a Muse Stream refresher (including a reminder of what to do if you get stuck)? Revisit the Muse Stream chapter in "Your Muse and You."*

- *Connect directly with your inner critic with the "Taming Your Inner Critic" meditation in Step #11.*

Exploration II • Your Muse Is Boss

You may believe that this creative project you're thinking about, working on or struggling over was your idea. It's probably more accurate to suggest that you were your Muse's idea. After all, it was your Muse that summoned you…that inspired you…that put the idea into your head.

So discard all notions that you're in charge. Abandon all pretense at control. You're not the boss. Your Muse is.

How did your Muse get to be boss? Because it's smarter than you are. Because it knows your creative projects and creative potential better than you do…than you ever will.

So you might as well forget everything you think you know about whatever it is you're working on, or will be working on, including all preconceptions about its form, structure and content.

Instead, listen to the voice of your Muse with an open heart and an open mind and approach all your creative projects from a place of surrender. Don't force your will onto them. Talk to them. Sit in the silence with them. Listen to them. Follow their lead. Let them have their way with you. If you do, they will create themselves for you.

Ask Yourself These Questions

Explore these questions in your Way of the Fool journal. Don't think about the answers, and don't feel as though you must answer each question individually if that doesn't feel right. It's okay to find your own way.

Let all your answers (or whatever single answer these questions trigger) emerge freely and honestly, writing them on the Muse Stream in a free-flowing, stream-of-consciousness way where appropriate.

- When it comes to my current creative project, where have I been acting as though I know best?
- Where have I been resisting my Muse's superior wisdom? Where have I been openly defying my Muse?
- What preconceptions about my creative project have I been clinging to? How can I let go some or all of them?
- Where have I been pushing my creative project rather than letting myself be pulled by it?
- Where in my relationship with my Muse and creative projects can I be more open-hearted? More trusting? More surrendered?
- In what other ways can I let my Muse be boss?

Creating on the Muse Stream

Revisit "Creating on the Muse Stream" from Step #1, and repeat the exercise.

When You're Finished…

How was this creative session different from others you have experienced? In process? In content? In emotional response? In resistance? Take a few minutes and note those differences, along with how the experience made you feel, in your Way of the Fool journal.

The Way of the Dreaming Fool

The voice of the Muse can make itself known in many ways. For Paul McCartney, it revealed itself in an unusual 1964 dream, during which he composed the entire melody of a new song. When McCartney woke the next morning, he rushed to the piano so he wouldn't forget it. Still, he was skeptical. Could he truly have come up with an original composition in a dream? Or had he subconsciously plagiarized an existing one?

As Craig Cross tells it in his 2005 book, *The Beatles: Day-by-Day, Song-by-Song, Record-by-Record*, McCartney spent the next month asking everyone he knew in the music business whether they had heard it before. No one had.

By mid-1965, his "dream melody" had morphed into the song "Yesterday," which became an instant hit when it was released later that year, topping the charts and selling a million copies within five weeks.

Named the number one pop song of all time in 2000 by *Rolling Stone* and MTV, "Yesterday" is now one of the most covered songs in the history of recorded music. It's also among the most profitable, having earned more than $30 million in royalties and publishing rights alone.

My Story: Coda I

My Muse Stream technique is like my leap of faith from the building of my nightmare: We let go of old structures (more willingly, one hopes, than I did in my meditation), and trust into the act of creation, knowing that the Muse will keep us safe.

Even so, when I began writing my first book, I wasn't certain the Muse Stream would work for a full-length creation. Until then, I had been using the technique, then a few years old, only to journal and for short vignettes.

The book, in fact, began life as just such a vignette, the result of a writing exercise in a Toronto workshop I was facilitating.

For the exercise, I had each student draw, closed-eyed, a major arcana card from a Celtic-inspired tarot deck. I then guided them on an open-eyed meditative journey based on their individual cards. From there, I had them write…on the Muse Stream, of course.

Until then, I had never written during one of my workshops. Instead, I would keep an eye on participants in case anyone needed my help. Yet something about this class was different: Some inner imperative — the voice of my Muse? — insisted I do the same exercise. So, with my eyes closed, I shuffled the remaining cards and picked one.

No, it wasn't the Fool. It was the Chariot.

I took a few minutes to study the card in the same way I had directed my students: from a holistic overview to a detailed study, and back to the overview. Then, without knowing what I was doing, I let the Muse Stream guide me into writing.

Nothing about my a rambling account of an odd-looking man in an odd-looking coach pulled by horses as oddly colored as those on the card made any sense to my logical mind. Why would it when I had neither plans nor a conscious desire to write a fantasy novel?

When the twenty minutes' writing time was up, I returned my focus to the workshop. I thought no more about my stranger and his horses until the next morning, when that same voice-of-my-Muse inner imperative urged me to reread what I'd written. Intrigued, I picked up my pen and continued from where I'd left off.

Was it a book? I didn't know. All I knew for certain was the chaotic jumble of characters and scenes I felt compelled to follow…that day, the next, then the next. Although it pushed all my control-issue buttons to keep going, to keep writing a story I knew nothing about, I persisted. I wrote on the Muse Stream every morning — generally before I got out of bed, to stop me from procrastinating the day away.

After a month and a half of this, my pages and pages of longhand scribblings[1] began to morph into something resembling a coherent narrative. It even had a title: *The MoonQuest*…not that I could identify where this *MoonQuest* was going or what the title signified.

Not yet.

Still, I had enough of a story that I had to keep writing — and trusting. I wrote daily, pausing only long enough to uproot my urban life in Toronto and replace it with one a thousand miles away in rural Nova Scotia. And a

---

[1] To forestall even more overwhelm, I would type each morning's longhand writing that evening, taking great care to prevent my hyper-judgmental mind from making any changes.

year to the day from the Chariot card in that workshop exercise, in a nondescript cottage by a saltwater marsh in tiny Amirault's Hill, I dropped the final period onto the final page of the first draft of *The MoonQuest*.

I had trusted my Muse, embraced the chaos and, to my amazement, written a novel.

My Story: Coda II

It took thirteen years, many more drafts and innumerable rejections before *The MoonQuest* found its way into print. Once it did, however, it went on to win six literary awards, spark feature-film interest and launch an ongoing, equally unexpected series, *The Legend of Q'ntana*.

I wrote each of those *Q'ntana* books, and all my other books, in much the same way I wrote *The MoonQuest*: trusting my Muse as, word-by-word, I took one Fool-ish leap of faith after the next until the story was done.

My Story: Coda III

Not long after my nightmare experience, I read something by Ray Bradbury where he said that, for him, writing was about leaping off cliffs and trusting that he would sprout wings on the way down. That's what I learned to do that winter morning all those years ago — in my creativity and my life.

In many ways, what Bradbury describes is the Way of the Creative Fool: that surrendered leap of faith into the Muse Stream that alchemically transforms into art something that, in the moment, appears to make no sense.

It can be a terrifying way to create. It can also be a terrifying way to live. It's especially terrifying when, each time I let go and trust my Muse/intuitive self, I'm that much closer to the pavement when the arms of God appear. Yet, like Bradbury's wings, that divine safety net has never failed to appear for me. Not once.

Declaration

I, *your name*, trust my Muse to open my heart and mind to the fullness and Fool-ness of my artistic gifts and to guide and direct me in the creation of my most dynamic and authentic work. And so it is.

Step #8. Free Your Creation

*It was as though the pastels were magic,
as though they possessed wills of their own
and his hand's only job was to hold
them up while they sketched.*
SARA'S YEAR, THE SARA STORIES, BOOK 1

Surrender to the creation that
has chosen you to birth it into the world.
Surrender to how it chooses to be birthed.
Surrender to the light of its superior wisdom.

Just as the Creator in most religious and spiritual
traditions allows you the free will to live your imperative
and forge your story through the living of it,
your highest call is to allow the creation
that leaps from your heart, mind and vision
that same freedom.

Your job as artist-creator is to let
the energy of your creation
emerge from formlessness into form
and to breathe life into it that it may experience
all it has come into your life to live...

that you may experience all
that you have joined with it to live.

Let there be light...and there will be.
Let your creation take form, and it will.

My Story

AFTER THE WORKSHOP experience I describe in Step #2, I could accept that *maybe* I was creative…when it came to writing. Beyond that? No way. I certainly wasn't a visual artist. After all, I could barely draw a stick figure, let alone any kind of competent artistic rendering.

Or could I…?

It's January 2004. I'm sitting in Lemuria Calling, the metaphysical store my wife and I own with another couple. With no customers around, I'm doodling absentmindedly, something I often do when bored or on the phone.

At least to me, these complex, rune-like jottings, scratched without thought onto any piece of paper with any pen, are doodles.

They aren't, however, to Courtney Eves, one of my spiritual mentors. Courtney is visiting Sedona from Connecticut and has stopped by the store. "Th-that's language of light," she sputters as she notices my inky scribbles. "That's incredible. It gives me goosebumps. Do you have any others?"

Language of light, a metaphysical term, can take many visual forms: calligraphic, runic, geometric, hieroglyphic or a blend of any of those. In an energetic-vibrational sense, it carries the same transformational potential as crystals, working subtly — sometimes not so subtly — at physical, emotional, spiritual and mental levels, touching places in our psyche far beneath the conscious mind.

Do I have other drawings? Of course, I don't. These are mindless squiggles. Why would I keep them?

"Is there an art store in town?" Courtney asks before I can respond.

"Uh, yes. Why?"

"Are you doing anything right now?"

"I—"

"Let's go."

As soon as we step into Sedona Art Supplies, Courtney hustles me to the colored pencils and has me choose a dozen. She then asks the sales clerk to pick out a suitable sketch pad and pays for the lot.

"Start drawing," she commands when we get back to Lemuria Calling.

I do, that afternoon.

Once I start, I can't stop. Not that day, the next or the next. I draw two, three, four, five drawings a day, from the simple to the complex, all from that non-thinking place that produced my doodles, drawing as intuitively as I write and sing.

Sing?

I may not have learned to sing in David Smukler's voice classes (see Step #3), but I was singing. Sort of.

Soon after I arrived in Sedona in 1997, I booked a session with Irlianna Samsara, a local sound healer. It was some of the most powerful energy work I had ever experienced…and among the most unnerving. That's because as I walked back to my car, I had the disturbing sense that I was being called to do similar work, making sounds at least as peculiar as those Irlianna had made during our time together.

For all my initial resistance, my brand of vocal sound work, distinct from Irlianna's, soon became part of the

Reiki-inspired attunements I was already offering. Not long after, sound became their focus. Always unusual and sometimes off-key, my "singing" ranged from grating to melodic, often carrying elements of Middle Eastern, Hawaiian and Native American tones and rhythms. I never knew what would come out of my mouth, and over time learned to trust that whatever I sang was perfect in the moment. As with writing *The MoonQuest*, it was a training in judgment-free surrender.

So was my drawing.

A few months after Courtney marched me into the art store, I began offering what I felt guided to call God Activations. Each of these teleconference events included a meditation, an inspirational talk and twenty minutes of light-language singing, all keyed to a topic or theme and all offered intuitively in the moment. I sold recordings of those events with great success, and when I added a light-language drawing for each, created just as intuitively, they became bestsellers as well.

To be honest, I had the most fun with drawings unrelated to my teleconference themes: interpretations — some vaguely realistic-looking, others more abstract — of the rock formations and other natural features I encountered on my travels. One of my favorites was of the Book Cliffs, the two-hundred-fifty-mile escarpment that straddles the Colorado-Utah state line.

It's still among my favorites, perhaps because it's the drawing that edged me back toward my primary creative passion: Within a few months of completing it, I also completed a final draft of *The MoonQuest*. A few months after that, I was holding an advanced copy of the book in my hands, and sobbing.

The Way of the Fool

The Fool rarely plans his journey or consults maps. Why plot itineraries when the most satisfying outings occur in the moment?

The Fool rarely identifies destinations. Why insist on a fixed outcome when the unconventional, the uncommon, the uncertain and the unexpected are responsible for all that is genuine, authentic and original?

The Fool does not expect the unexpected, for the Fool has no expectations. The Fool flies into the unexpected. The Fool dives into the unexpected. The Fool relishes the unexpected.

The Way of Fool is the unimagined and the unimaginable, the undefined and the indefinable, the unconceived and the inconceivable.

The Fool colors outside the lines and frees up experiences that are distinctive and authentic. More accurately, the Fool rejects coloring books altogether, preferring the blank canvas of total faith and unfettered freedom.

Ongoing, unconditional faith is the Way of the Fool. When we surrender to it, we free ourselves to discover a path never before traveled, a path uniquely our own.

Your Story

Exploration • The Language of Creation

One of the most eloquent ways we express how we feel about ourselves and our creative work, even as we're rarely aware we're doing it, is through our words and thoughts. Too often, those words and thoughts are dismissive, denigrating or disdainful.

For example, when it comes to issues around our creativity, we commonly use language like "can't," "impossible," "too hard," "not ready," "not good enough," "not enough time/skill/talent/creativity," "don't dare," "don't know how" or "blocked."

What are we owning about ourselves and our creativity when we use words and phrases like that? What are we reinforcing?

Try this… Without censoring yourself, pay attention to your language over the next seventy-two hours. Not the language you write. The language you speak. Listen for the words and phrases that reveal — sometimes subtly, sometimes with alarming clarity — what it is you feel, what it is you fear, what it is you judge.

Again, don't censor yourself. And don't beat yourself up when you notice yourself using language that's diminishing or judgmental. Rather, listen for those words and phrases, learn from them and find ways to replace them with language that's more affirming and respectful. Be the Creative Fool you are.

For now, here's a selection of the more common disempowering words and phrases you might hear yourself saying…

- **Block** *or* **Blocked** — *As in "I'm blocked creatively."* You're not.

- **Impossible** — *Any use, unless preceded by the word "not."* You are an innately creative being of infinite potential. Nothing is impossible.

- **I'm Not** — *Any use that involves unfavorable comparisons with what others are, have created or have accomplished.* Any "I'm not" negates a part of you. Replace your I'm nots with I ams, and let each "I am" be a declaration of empowerment that braces, bolsters and buttresses your self-esteem, your creativity, your creative expression and your creative enterprise.

- **Not As Good As** *or* **Not As Much As** — *Any use that involves unfavorable comparisons with what others are, have accomplished or have created.* You don't have to create like anyone else. You don't want to create like anyone else. The world isn't waiting for another [insert your favorite creative artist's name]. The world waits for you. You and your unique perspective. You and your unique world view. You and your unique way of expressing things. You and your creativity. Comparison is nothing more than an excuse to put yourself down. Instead, raise yourself up. Celebrate who you are and where you are. Experience the masters. Learn from the masters. Then be the master you are. (See Step #12.)

- **Not Enough** — *As in, "not good enough" or "not creative enough" or "not enough time" or "not enough talent."* There is always enough, and you are always enough. Period. Don't subscribe to lack in any aspect of your life. Embrace abundance and the abundant, and embrace the abundantly creative being you are.

- **Hard** *or* **Difficult** *or* **Challenging** — *As in, "It's hard because…" or "It's difficult to…" or "It's challenging to…"* Give no energy to negativity or perceived difficulty. Just do it. Be the Creative Fool you are.

- **Pointless** *or* **Futile** *or* **Waste** — *As in, "What I'm creating is pointless" or "This is futile" or "This is a waste of time/effort."* There is no such thing as a wasted creative act, action, project or enterprise. Every creative act, action, project or enterprise is part of the necessary journey that carries you to the next, and to the next one after that.

- **Just** *or* **Only** — *As in, "This is just a journal entry" or "This is just a first draft/sketch/attempt" or "This is just for me" or "I'm only a…" or "I've spent only fifteen minutes or fifty or five on my creative project today/this week…" or "I've only produced…" or "This is just crap."* Don't belittle who you are and what you have already achieved. Celebrate every achievement and milestone, regardless of how small it seems to your critical mind. (See Step #12.)

- **Control** — *As in, "I must control this story/project" or "I need to control this process" or "I have to control my characters/plot/brushstrokes/output."* Abandon control. You're not in charge, and any thoughts that you might be are illusion…or delusion.

- **Has to Be** — *As in, "This has to be a certain genre" or "This has to look/sound/be expressed a certain way."* Your Muse knows your project's length/form/medium/optimal expression. Trust it.

- **Order** *or* **Sequence** — *As in, "I need to write/create this in a particular order" or "I have to create this in a certain sequence."* Surrender to your Muse's superior wisdom and let your creative expression/project emerge as it chooses to emerge, not as you would have it emerge.

- **Trying** — *As in, "I'm trying to make time for my creativity" or "I'm trying to work on my creative project every day."* To quote Yoda: "Do or do not. There is no try." Set goals you know you can meet, and meet them. (See Step #10.)

- **Can't** *or* **Cannot** *or* **Don't Dare** — *In any context.* There is nothing you cannot create, say, do or be. Stop judging yourself. Stop limiting yourself. Start being yourself.

- **Problem** — *In any context.* There is no difficulty in your creative life or anywhere else in your life that does not carry within it the seeds of opportunity. Even if the opportunity seems invisible in the moment, trust in its existence and shift your focus from the apparent negative to the always-present potential for a redemptive outcome.

- **Supposed to** *or* **Have to** *or* **Must** *or* **Must Not** — *In any context.* Where do your "supposed tos," "have-tos" and "must nots" come from? A teacher? A parent? A spouse? A sibling? A friend? A boss? A colleague? A fellow creative artist? Don't look outside yourself for guidance or validation. Go within. Listen to your heart. Listen to your work. Listen to your Muse. Listen to the infinite mind that holds within it the wisdom of the universe and that lives within you, always.

- **Should** — *In any context.* Have you ever noticed that the word "shoulder" begins with the word "should"? Have you ever noticed how much tension you carry in your shoulders? Un-should yourself and feel the burdens that you have allowed others to place on your shoulders melt away. (Revisit the "No More Shoulds" meditation in Step #1.)

Now, focus instead on these words and phrases...

- **Surrender** — Can you surrender to whatever you are creating? To the creative imperative underlying it? Can you surrender to your Muse? To the projects it would have you create?

- **Release** *and* **Let Go** — Can you let go all thoughts that limit you and hold you back? Can you release the reins on your creativity? On your life?

- **Fly Free** *and* **Unlimited** — Can you let yourself fly free? Can you see your creative potential as unlimited?

- **Leap of Faith** — To launch any act of creative expression requires a leap of faith. How about taking one of those leaps, right now?

How about *trust*? Or *allow*? Or *I can*? Or *I will*? How about *possible* or *doable* or *now*?

How about focusing on what you have accomplished, not on what is lacking from your work? How about reminding yourself that you are a creator...and a powerful one?

How about remembering that everything is not only possible, but as easy as you will allow it to be?

As you do that, you will birth more creative excellence than you could ever produce by worrying, judging, diminishing or deriding.

Listen to your words. Hear what they tell you about

what you think and believe. Then, without censoring yourself, begin to transform the limiting thoughts and beliefs they represent into affirming, empowering ones. Believe in you!

Meditation: The Butterfly

Have your Way of the Fool journal handy to record your thoughts, feelings and impressions. Allow at least 20 minutes for this experience. Allow additional time after the meditation if you plan further explorations — in your journal or through creative expression.

My studio recording of "The Butterfly," one nearly identical to this version, is available for download or streaming[1] as part of "The Voice of the Muse Companion: Guided Meditations for Writers."

Revisit "Getting Started" to find out how to access the recording, as well as for tips on how best to use this book's meditations, visualizations and meditative journeys.

Close your eyes. Breathe in deeply, fully. Allow your shoulders to drop, then drop some more. And some more. Allow yourself to relax. Fully.

From that place of calm, let your breath transport you into the realm of imagination, the realm of creativity, the realm of vision.

See yourself now in another form, another body. A caterpillar's body.

You're a caterpillar, enfolded in a cocoon.

Like a blanket-bundled infant or your blanket-bundled sleep-in self, you're enveloped in the gentle, divine caress of in-between time.

In this moment, you're safe. Safe in the all-embracing

---
[1] Search the relevant site/store for "Mark David Gerson butterfly."

darkness. Secure in the womb of creation, transformation, rebirth.

Creation. Transformation. Rebirth.

Feel that transformation within you. Feel your shape begin to shift. Feel your body lighten and wings begin to form.

Feel the nascent emergence of color, translucence, delicacy.

Now, feel the pressure of your wings as, pressed between your body and the walls of the cocoon, they push and spread, push and spread.

Push and spread.

Such delicate wings, yet so strong.

So strong.

Such a delicate body, yet so strong.

So strong.

So awake. So determined. So ready.

What was once a sanctuary is now stifling. What once held you in safety now presses against you, holds you down. Holds you back.

Thank the cocoon and the caterpillar you were for letting you sleep, for keeping you safe, for holding you secure. Thank them and release them from the need to do so any longer.

Now it's time to awaken.

Now it's time to fly.

Now it's time to be a creature of earth and sky. Of sky and earth.

Now it's time to travel great distances, to soar to great heights, to stretch the limits of the possible. To enter into the realm of the improbable, the realm of the impossible.

Feel the walls of your cocoon give way. Feel your wings spread as they push and push and push some more.

It's hard work, at times, to push free of the barriers

we have created for ourselves. But we always have the strength. We always have the will.

We always have the power.

All we need to do is acknowledge our strength, surrender to our highest imperative, and allow our power to have its way with us.

It's time to surrender. To the butterfly you are. To the creator you are.

To the free-flowing, free-flying being you are.

So do it.

Push one last time with those wings that seem so delicate but carry the strength and will of the universe. Push one last time and feel the walls of your cocoon break apart.

Now, spread your wings to the fullness of their span and fly free.

Fly free.

Fly free.

Now.

You may feel tentative, uncertain. Shaky. That's normal. These are new wings, new experiences, new expressions. Allow the uncertainty, knowing that with each flight you will become more certain, more practiced, more adept.

Fly for as long as you like. Explore your new world from this new perspective. Take your time. And when you're ready to light down again — on a flower petal, on a leaf or on a blank sheet of paper that has fluttered to earth — open your eyes and write about your experiences, your feelings, your journey.

Write about them as the caterpillar-turned-butterfly. Describe your transformation, your liberation, your flight.

And write about them as the creator you are, now free of one more barrier to your freest, fullest expression.

Alternatively, use another creative medium to describe your experience and express the feelings it evoked.

Try This

Consider making some unique variation of the word "butterfly" or the phrase "I am a butterfly" as the username for a frequently used login. Repeatedly typing a statement like that will help reinforce it for you.

Creating on the Muse Stream

Revisit "Creating on the Muse Stream" from Step #1, and repeat the exercise.

When You're Finished…

How was this creative session different from others you have experienced? In process? In content? In emotional response? In resistance? Take a few minutes and note those differences, along with how the experience made you feel, in your Way of the Fool journal.

The Way of the Surrendered Fool

Annie was in her late fifties when she attended her first class of mine. Short, with close-cropped graying hair, she had a pixie's frame but lacked a pixie's spark.

"I want to write a memoir," she declared when we introduced ourselves, each word measured, controlled. "But I have writer's block. I have had it for a decade."

Annie struggled with the early exercises, struggled against the controls she had placed on her self-expression. She wanted to avoid going where her pen was taking her, wanted to force her pen in other directions.

Yet once she surrendered to her pen and freed that pixie part of herself that was now, at last, finding expression, she had everyone in the room laughing so hard at the absurdities of her Earth Mother alter ego that we couldn't stop crying.

Annie, and that's not her real name, didn't have writer's block. She was afraid to free and embrace the part of herself that was light, funny, bizarre and uncontrollable. Once she did, her self-described block dissolved in a rush of daily writing — simply for the pleasure of seeing where it would take her, just for the joy of creation.

My Story: Coda

It's July 2024, nearly twenty years since the last of my light-language events. I haven't picked up my colored pencils in over a decade, and the only sound work I have done through much of that time has been for myself. Nearly all my focus since *The MoonQuest*'s 2007 release has been on writing more books…twenty-two more, to be precise, with several others in-progress.

As I open my eyes to this summer morning, however, writing isn't on my mind. My light-language drawings are.

Could it be time to revive that aspect of my creative and metaphysical work? I'm skeptical, not least because all my art supplies are stuffed into a storage unit two hundred fifty miles away.

Wait! This is 2024. I don't need colored pencils. I don't need a sketch pad. I have an iPad loaded with Procreate, a drawing app.

I watch a few Procreate tutorials, then try my hand — literally — at some finger painting. As with my earlier pencil efforts, I draw whatever wants to be freed…this time, onto the screen. What emerges is radically different from my drawings of eleven years ago…and radically more powerful. Everyone I show them to agrees.

As I wait for the Apple Pencil I've ordered, I dig deep into the app and discover the coolest feature imaginable: Procreate records a time-lapse of the drawing as I'm drawing it, then saves that time-lapse as a video.

I'm not only creating static drawings. I'm animating video shorts!

Then, a brainstorm. What if I were to add a soundtrack to each animation? What if *I* were to add a soundtrack…to *sing* a soundtrack…to treat the animated glyphs and runes as a musical score? If my logical mind doesn't know what I'm drawing, my Muse through my intuitive mind does. I will free it to sing the score.

The results are astounding — visually, vocally and energetically. Moreover, even people not normally sensitive to crystals are experiencing physical and emotional shifts when they watch the videos.

As with my colored-pencil drawings, I can't stop. Every day I create a new "sound drawing," or more than one. Before long, I'm selling these on my website alongside my books and writing courses.

I could never have created any of these with my logical mind. Not the drawings, not the sounds, not the animated blend of the two. But, as I do with my writing, I can get out of my own way, surrender to the voice of my Muse and free creation to create itself.

Declaration

I, *your name*, listen nonjudgmentally to the voice of my Muse, surrender unconditionally to its innate wisdom and trust it, fully and Fool-ly, to activate my highest creative expression. As the Creative Fool that I am, I free my creations to create themselves — naturally and spontaneously on the Muse Stream. And so it is.

Step #9. Strive for Excellence, Not Perfection

Perfection is no more possible in your creativity than it is in your life, so embrace the perfect imperfection of both your art and your humanity. Strive for excellence, not perfection.
THE VOICE OF THE MUSE: ANSWERING THE CALL TO WRITE

In nature, perfection arrives
in the instant preceding the start of decay.

In nature, perfection breathes but a single breath,
barely surviving the span of a lone heartbeat.

In nature, perfection signals
the beginning of the end...of everything.

There is no success beyond perfection.
There is no future beyond perfection.
There is no creation beyond perfection.

There is no
life beyond perfection.

There is nothing
beyond perfection.

There is everything beyond excellence.
Worlds of possibility. Galaxies of possibility.
Infinite realms of possibility.

The pursuit of excellence frees you to keep growing.
The pursuit of excellence frees you to keep learning.
The pursuit of excellence frees you to keep creating.
The pursuit of excellence frees you to keep succeeding.

Strive for excellence, not perfection.

My Story

IT'S MID-1994, and I have been working as a full-time writer and editor for eighteen years. I'm good at my job, and I have an active client list that ranges from book and magazine publishers to universities, government agencies and corporate communications departments. You have to be good to make it as a freelancer, which I have been doing successfully for more than a decade, most of it in the highly competitive Toronto market.

I can't do it anymore. Not the editing part. I can no longer spend my days as a professional perfectionist. I can no longer live my work life largely from my left brain, not when I'm trying to live the rest of my life more holistically…not when I'm seeking ways to be more creative in my personal and writing pursuits.

By October 1994 I have wrapped up all my current jobs, let go all my editing clients and retreated a thousand miles away from the hyper-bustle of Canada's largest city to the hyper-stillness of rural Nova Scotia.

There, I apply the free-flow writing technique I have not yet dubbed "the Muse Stream" to completing the first draft of my first novel. It is as I settle into the radical rewrite that is *The MoonQuest*'s second draft six months later that I experience the glimmerings of a new approach to editing. It's a groundbreaking approach that runs counter to all the ways I have practiced the craft…to everything I think I know about the craft.

It's about getting out of my finicky, detail-oriented head and into my heart, which is also the heart of the story. It's about listening, not pushing. It's about recognizing that not only does this draft not have to be perfect, it can't be perfect. It's about doing the best as the writer I am today and letting that be okay.

The Way of the Fool

Every effort the Fool makes is her best effort. Every step the Fool takes is his best step. Every word the Fool utters is her best expression. Yet no effort he makes, step he takes or word he speaks is perfect.

Does she judge herself for these many imperfections? He does not.

The Fool judges no effort as inadequate, no step as not good enough, no means of expression as deficient. The Fool does not judge.

The Fool recognizes that perfection does not and cannot exist. More significant still, the Fool knows that perfection could never be an appealing objective even were it possible, for beyond perfection lies a lifeless void.

Instead, the Fool does her best in each moment.

That "best" is always good enough because the Fool never holds back from fear of judgment or feelings of inadequacy, and because he knows the next moment will bring with it a more accomplished effort and more outstanding outcome.

The Fool sees the perfection in all imperfection and celebrates the unfolding journey of wisdom, growth, maturity that is the Way of the Fool.

Your Story

There's a difference between striving for excellence and striving for perfection. The first is attainable, gratifying and healthy. The second is often unattainable, frustrating and neurotic.
EDWIN BLISS, MANAGEMENT CONSULTANT

Embrace Imperfection • I

Your work may be excellent, accomplished, creative and insightful. It may be innovative and compelling. It may be brilliant. But perfect? Not possible.

It's not possible because when we translate an idea or concept into some form of creative expression, we're taking something infinite (energy) and dynamic (neural impulses) and converting it into something finite and static.

Perfection is not possible in any creative endeavor.
Perfection is not possible in any human endeavor.
It's simply not possible.

Try This

Can you let go of your natural human perfectionism long enough to free your creation to reveal itself to you? To create itself? To create you? What are you waiting for? Pick up the tools of your artistry and let creation have its way with you. Don't try to be perfect. Don't try at all. Allow.

And know that from that place of surrender, you can't but create the nearest thing possible to perfection.

Embrace Imperfection • II

It's when we judge ourselves or our creative work to be not good enough that we strive to be perfect.

After all, if we can manage to be perfect, no one can judge or shame us. Right?

Use the questions that follow to explore what perfection means to you. Don't think about your answers. Instead, open your Way of the Fool journal and use the Muse Stream to journey into the heart of the matter. Record any emotions the questions trigger and any experiences they bring to the surface, as well as whatever emerges through your free-flow, free-of-conscious-thought writings.

- In what ways do I judge myself to be not good enough? Physically? Professionally? Athletically? Sexually? Creatively? Any other ways?

- What does perfection mean to me?

- In which areas of my life and/or creative work do I find myself striving to be perfect?

- Is there an area of my life and/or creative work where I am most insecure and strive most for perfection? What is it? Why is it so important to me? When did it start being so important? Which person or persons, event or events, triggered that perceived importance?

- What do I fear would be the consequences of not being "perfect" in my life and/or creativity? Fear aside, what would the *real* consequences, if any, be?

- What does it mean to me to "do my best" with my creative work? In other areas of my life?
- Can I allow my "best" work/efforts to not be perfect? If so, how would that feel? If I can't, why not?

A Few More Questions…

Explore these questions as well, and don't think about the answers. Let them emerge freely and honestly…on the Muse Stream, where appropriate:

- In my creative work, do I strive for excellence? Or do I neurotically seek perfection? *If it's the former, keep up the good work and find a way to celebrate the achievement (see Step #12). If the latter, spend extra time with Step #9, and give yourself permission to embrace imperfection.*
- Do I judge what I create to be not good enough? Not good enough for what? For whom? *If so, notice your judgments, don't judge yourself for them and do your best to keep going — through and past your judgment. Need help? That's what the next guided meditation is for.*

Meditation: Let Judgment Go

Have your Way of the Fool journal handy to record your thoughts, feelings and impressions. Allow at least 30 minutes for this experience, longer if you plan further explorations in your journal once you have completed the meditation.

My studio recording of "Let Judgment Go," one nearly identical to this version, is available for download or streaming[1] as part of "The Voice of the Muse Companion: Guided Meditations for Writers."

Revisit "Getting Started" to find out how to access the recording, as well as for tips on how best to use this book's meditations, visualizations and meditative journeys.

Breathe. Breathe in the quiet, white light of your creative essence, your divine essence, your Muse.

Breathe in your fire, your flame, your beingness, your God-self.

Breathe in the light of who you are, the truth of who you are, the love of who you are.

Breathe in all the light and aloha you are.

Aloha is not merely a word that conjures up the gentle swaying of palm trees and hula dancers. Aloha is a consciousness, a state of being, a state of openheartedness, a state of love in its truest, fullest sense.

Breathe in to that openness within you. Breathe it in fully, deeply, completely.

Breathe out any doubts, any fears that you're not good enough, that someone else or anyone else — your friend who has already been published, your neighbor whose art is hanging in galleries, your creative colleague who has won awards for her work — is a more accomplished artist. Breathe that out, for it is not true.

You are creative. You are innately creative. You are inherently creative. Everyone is. And because you are, you can express that creativity through your innate gifts.

Let go of all feelings that you're not good enough. For you are. Release all feelings that others are better than you. They are not. You are equal to all and equal to the joyful task at hand, which is expressing the passions of your heart in creative form.

---

[1] Search the relevant site/store for "Mark David Gerson let judgment go."

You are equal to it, for you were born to it. Every micro-bit, every nano-bit of your being — physical, emotional and spiritual — has been encoded with that will, desire and aptitude to create.

You may lack certain skills. Those skills can be learned and practiced. In this moment, skills don't matter nearly as much as heart, intent and choice. You have the former. We all do. And you can tap into the latter two with ease.

Know that and be that.

It's simple. It's simple yet complex, for you are pushing against what may seem like lifetimes of programming.

What has been programmed can be erased — more quickly than the time it took to program into you.

You are good enough. You are better than good enough.

Despite what anyone ever said, despite any way in which you were treated — words and actions your conscious mind may have long ago forgotten or buried — despite any or all of these, you are a creator, a creative artist.

You are good enough. Your work is good enough. Your creations are good enough. Better than good enough. For they are the unique expressions of a unique heart that is even now opening to the prospect and possibility of finally being free to express itself…to the prospect and possibility of transcending all perfectionism.

Feel that freedom. Open to that freedom. Embrace that freedom. It needn't frighten you. It needn't shut you down. It is safe. For in that freedom lies all the truth of the universe, just as within you lies all the truth of the universe.

So do your best with all your creations. Whatever you set out to create, strive for the excellence that is encoded into your soul, not for the perfection that is unattainable… not solely for you, but for everyone.

So let go into your best efforts — your truly best efforts

— and trust that in so doing, you will sparkle and shine, that you will radiate and be radiant. That you will excel. That you do excel.

Creation is an act of allowing, of letting. "Let there be light," the God of the Old Testament said. Not, "I order and command light." Not, "The light must look a certain way, must be a certain brightness." God *allowed* light, allowed the world to form.

Let there be light. Let there be creation. Let there be one world, then another. And let the creations that best express those worlds find their own way out of you and, from you, into the larger world.

Let. Let your creations be. Let yourself be.

There is no judging in the act of letting. There is no call to judge. There is no call to take any active role whatsoever. Surrender to creation and let it be.

God didn't say as the earth formed, "You know, I don't like this island over here and that mountain over there." God allowed the earth to form and saw it, *and it was good*. God didn't judge it to be good. By allowing, it was good. Inherently good.

Allow your creations to form without judgment and they, too, will be good. Give your creations life. Then give them the free will to form as they will, to live their imperative.

Let.

Let them form.

Let them be.

Let them love you.

Let yourself love them back.

There is no need to judge. There is never any need to judge. The only call is to let. The only call is to be. The only call is to create.

So let yourself be. Let yourself create. Let yourself do

your best. Let yourself excel. Let yourself be good enough. For you are.

What does that feel like? How do you feel now that you have let judgment go? Do you feel lighter? Freer? Open your Way of the Fool journal and explore that lightness, that freedom. Explore your new path to excellence.

Creating on the Muse Stream

Now that you have let judgment go, revisit "Creating on the Muse Stream" from Step #1, and repeat the exercise.

When You're Finished...

How was this creative session different from others you have experienced? Did you feel less self-critical? Less judgmental? Any other noticeable differences? In process? In content? In emotional response? In resistance? Take a few minutes and note those differences, along with how the experience made you feel, in your Way of the Fool journal.

The Way of the Perfectionist Fool

Long fascinated by Napoleon, filmmaker Stanley Kubrick leveraged the commercial success of his *2001: A Space Odyssey* (not to mention its five Oscar nominations) into $420,000[2] in development funds from MGM for his next venture: an ambitious biopic about the French emperor.

An obsessive perfectionist, Kubrick was determined to portray every element of Napoleon's life with painstaking accuracy. He sent researchers across Europe to gather material. He collected 276 books, many of which he annotated with asterisks, underlinings and notes. He put together a library-style card catalog so exhaustive that it allowed him to access everything from what Napoleon ate for breakfast to what wife Josephine wore to dinner *on any given day*. He amassed a comprehensive picture file of some fifteen thousand entries, organized by subject and encyclopedically cross-indexed to facilitate access by anyone on the production design team.

Kubrick also dispatched his assistant to Paris to bring back whatever he could find that was associated with Napoleon. Among the retrieved treasures was soil from the site of the Battle of Waterloo. Kubrick wanted to ensure that wherever the iconic battle was ultimately shot, his team would be able to match precisely the color and texture

---

[2] $3.9 million in 2025 dollars.

of the earth of the original battleground. The assistant also found and brought back Napoleon's portable toilet.

Kubrick was so invested in his subject that he was said to have adopted Napoleon's habit of mixing main course and dessert foods as he ate.

Finally, after two years of all-consuming preproduction planning, Kubrick had a script, a schedule and a budget. The perfectionist was ready to proceed.

MGM wasn't. While Kubrick was obsessing, the studio had lost interest in the project.

The film was never made.

My Story: Coda

Another decade passes, and I'm editing again — for others as well as for myself; no longer from that narrow-focused, analytical place that built my earlier professional success, but from that heartful, whole-brain place I have been cultivating since that second draft of *The MoonQuest*.

A book on editing has been on my to-do list for much of that time. Yet although I now practice this technique with great success on my work and my clients' and although I teach the occasional workshop on the subject, I feel as though I am missing the key that will make it possible for me to guide others with the kind of depth that a full-length book demands.

Then the covid pandemic strikes, forcing me to recreate all my classes for an online-only audience. As I put together my newly reimagined revision workshop, I have a sudden flash of insight: I have found my key. *Keys*, rather. Three of them: vision, intuition and excellence (not perfection).

As with so many of our aha moments, I'm stunned that I failed to recognize the significance of those elements before now. The cliché "hidden in plain sight" leaps to mind because those three words are already integral to all my creative work. They also differentiate my editing philosophy from most others.

Without vision, there is no global creative concept for the many and myriad editorial changes every writing project requires.

Without intuition, we edit mechanically, soullessly and without discernment, something a computer or an AI bot could easily manage more effectively.

And without stressing excellence over perfection, we lose ourselves in a quest for the impossible.

A year later, I complete and publish *The Heartful Art of Revision: An Intuitive Guide to Editing*. Is it the perfect book on editing? Definitely not. But it's pretty damn good!

Declaration

I, *your full name*, commit to my best efforts in all I create. As the Fool that I am, I strive for excellence in all my endeavors, freeing my creative expression to flow into its idea of perfection, not mine. And so it is.

Step #10. Commit to Your Passion

*Now is the time to
put your dreams into action.*
ORGANIC SCREENWRITING:
WRITING FOR FILM, NATURALLY

What does commitment mean?
It means making your creativity a priority in your life.

It means not letting fear, excuses or distractions
divert you from listening for the voice of your Muse
and surrendering to its call.

It means letting the ideas of your heart
find expression through your mind.

It means trusting your Muse to know the way
and to guide you from conception to completion.

It means honoring your passion
and respecting yourself.

One thing is certain:
Unless or until you free the voice of your Muse
to live through you, you will not be free —
in your creativity or in your life.

My Story

It's a fall afternoon in 1980. Montreal's oaks and maples have already burst into fiery display, and a chill has begun to cut into the city's balmy Indian summer. Gripping his ever-present cup of coffee, my boss motions me to follow him into his office.

"Close the door," he says furtively.

David's windowless burrow crackles with electricity, as though its heavy wooden beams anticipate the great revelation that is about to unfold. He doesn't smile as he settles himself behind his desk and motions for me to sit. Yet his eyes are bright with excitement.

"I have a plan," he announces, "and you're part of it." He grins. "A big part."

I edge forward. My jaw tenses. I fidget.

I have worked in Concordia University's public relations department for four years and have advanced quickly, from information officer to assistant PR director. I'm also editor of the university's weekly newspaper. And I'm barely twenty-six.

It's a good job, though not without its stresses, and I have learned a lot, thanks in large measure to David Allnutt. Only six years my senior, the handsome, curly-haired wunderkind came to Concordia a few years ago from Quebec City. There, he served as executive assistant to the previous Quebec premier and chief of staff to three of his senior cabinet ministers. He was hired with a mandate to professionalize our reactive information office into a proactive PR department that would capitalize on his government connections.

"I want to expand this office from a public relations department to a public affairs department that would encompass PR, government relations…and much more." David leans forward, an aura of empire-building surrounding him. "I want you to take over as PR director. You would still report to me, but you would be in charge of all this." He indicates the warren of offices and alcoves that is now his realm alone. "I have it all worked out, but I want you on board before I present it to the Rector."

David continues talking — about the intricacies of his plan and his strategy for getting it approved. All I hear is the occasional word. My deafness isn't daydreaming anticipation. It's anxious foreboding. My nervous stomach pinches, and I wondered if I have any Maalox left in my desk drawer.

I had no insightful inner life in those days, and I was more than five years from any kind of spiritual awareness. Then, whatever intuitive guidance system operating within me kept a low profile. A few years later, it would urge me to move to Toronto. This October day, it flashed an alarming array of warning lights at me. I knew I should have been excited. This was an unparalleled opportunity for advancement. Sure, the university was struggling against a regime of funding cuts that had inflated workloads and deflated salary expectations.

Yet that was an argument in favor of David's ideas. Montreal's youngest English-language university needed better relations with a French-language government committed to pulling Quebec out of Canada, a government that was the source of most of the institution's budget.

David, with his influential contacts in the provincial capital, was well-placed to spearhead that transformation.

And yet…

And yet without understanding why, I knew this was the last thing I wanted.

As the days passed, I tried to be as equivocal with David as I could be. Meantime, I edged closer and closer to resigning. The only way I could describe it to friends was that I felt as though my career was being hijacked, as though it was pulling me in a wrong direction. It felt illogical, ridiculous…even stupid, as I couldn't identify a "right" direction. At the same time, I was unable to shake the feeling that accepting David's offer would be the worst mistake of my life.

A few weeks later, I quit. I would freelance until I could figure out my next step. My Muse had turned me into a full-time writer.

The Way of the Fool

In the world of the Fool, passion is all there is. There is no moment when he is uncommitted, unenthusiastic or half-hearted. There is no instant when she is detached, disengaged or disconnected. He refuses to acknowledge the unoriginal, the uninspired, the unimaginative. She cannot imagine herself as disheartened, discouraged or dispirited. The Fool embraces each day with delight…dives into every encounter with gusto…leaps into each undertaking with wholehearted fervor.

The Way of the Fool is not an occasional pursuit or part-time path. The Fool does not relegate his passion to nights and weekends or to disjointed fragments of "free time." Each breath is breathed with passion. Each step is taken with passion. Each word is spoken with passion. Each thought is steeped in passion. Each action is informed by passion. Each creation is inspired by passion. There is no moment, waking or sleeping, during which passion is not her compass, does not light her way.

When you commit to your passion, create from that passion, live your passion and free your passion to live through you, you walk the Way of the Fool.

Your Story

Exploration I • Time to Create

Too often we labor under the false assumption that we have no time to devote to our creativity, that our lives are too busy with work, family or other responsibilities. "I'll wait until the kids grow up and move out," we say. Or, "I'll do it when I retire." Why wait until more than half your life is over to start living your creativity dreams?

I'm here to tell you that you *do* have time for your creativity, even in the midst of the overwhelming calendar of obligations and commitments we all juggle every day. How do you find that time? By becoming conscious of the ways you now spend your time.

For each of the following activities, estimate (*honestly*) a weekly average in your Way of the Fool journal. Why weekly? Because for most of us, not all days are created equal. (Don't worry: I'm not going to ask you to give up any of these pursuits.)

How much time each week do you spend…

1. Watching movies, TV and streaming video, alone or with friends/family?

2. On social media (not including time spent posting content to promote your creative work)?

3. Listening to podcasts?

4. Playing video and/or other online games?

5. Out to dinner, coffee and/or drinks with friends/family?

6. Reading for pleasure, online or in print, including books, newspapers, magazines and blogs?

7. On nonessential research, including random Googling and/or browsing?

8. At movies, galleries and other cultural activities?

9. At live theater (not including shows your kids, other family members or close friends are performing in)?

10. At sporting/athletic events (not including those your kids, other family members or close friends are competing in)?

11. At bars and clubs?

12. At the gym?

13. On other nonessential pursuits and activities, online or off?

14. Traveling and commuting (not in a vehicle you're driving)?

I promised I wouldn't force you to sacrifice any activities unrelated to your creativity. So here's what I want you to do. Take each of your totals and divide it by half; one half stays with the activity, and the sum of the remaining halves is allocated to creative pursuits.

Can you free up that time every week to devote to your creativity in some way? No? What if you were to divide your weekly totals differently, devoting only a third of that time to creative pursuits? A quarter? Ten percent?

Note that when it comes to #14 (travel/commuting), there is nothing to give up. If your creative pursuit supports it, all I ask is that you dedicate some of that travel time to your creativity. No, you can't garden, cook or build furniture in a plane, train, taxi or subway. But you can write. You can sketch. You can brainstorm. You can do a journaling exercise from *The Way of the Creative Fool*. You can read books and articles or watch videos related to your form or medium.

Ask Yourself These Questions

Explore these questions in your Way of the Fool journal. Let your answers emerge freely and honestly, writing them on the Muse Stream in a free-flowing, stream-of-consciousness way where appropriate:

- How can I make creativity a priority in my life?
- What's my realistic commitment to my creativity?
- How much time will I devote to my creativity today? Tomorrow? Next week?

Exploration II • Into the Heart of Discipline

"What about discipline?" you ask. "Everything I read and hear says I'll never start (let alone finish) a creative project without discipline."

I'm glad you asked.

Let's start with the word "discipline." Its primary definition in *The Oxford English Dictionary* goes like this: "the practice of training people to obey rules or a code of behavior, using punishment to correct disobedience." Then there are the word's origins: from the Middle English, meaning "mortification by scourging oneself."

Punishment? Disobedience? Mortification? Scourging? Is that how you choose to experience your creativity?

Yes, most books, courses and so-called gurus equate productivity and success with discipline. The problem is that they define discipline, *Oxford*-like, as an ironclad routine chained to some measure of productivity.

That's not how I view discipline. As I see it, there are two types a creative artist can adopt: conventional or "hard" discipline, or what I call "heart" discipline.

Hard discipline, as *Oxford* suggests, is unyielding, punishing and rule-bound, threatening creative catastrophe should you stray from a rigorous routine. Hard discipline is disempowering and mistrustful because it implies that you lack the commitment to create and the discernment to know when to create. Hard discipline makes it easy to feel shamed, less-than, not-good-enough and blocked.

Heart discipline is different. Heart discipline fosters discernment, intuition and practice. Heart discipline nurtures passion and commitment. Heart discipline knows no fixed rules, times or goals. Heart discipline is fluid and in-the-moment. Heart discipline places your Muse, your creative projects and your passion in charge of your creative enterprise.

Heart discipline says trust. Trust that when you settle into a creative session, whenever that is, your Muse will be there for you. Trust that all you hear, including that it is either time to start a creative session or time to stop, is true. Trust that whatever flows through you on a given day is perfect, whatever the objective output.

Heart discipline is about discipleship. It's about you becoming a disciple — to your passion, to your Muse, to your creativity. It is not about forcing a creative vision that is boundless in nature to hew to the constraints of a controlling mind or be constricted by a conventional wisdom that is inevitably more conventional than it is wise.

Like intuition and discernment, trust is a practice.

Practice listening to what's inside you — to the voice of your Muse, the voice of your passion, the voice of your vision, the voice of your project — not to the judgmental, fear-based voices clamoring inside your head or to the disciplinary voices preaching at you from everywhere else. (Need help? Revisit "Your Story" in Step #7.)

What if you have no passion for your creative project? Then it's probably not the right project for you for right now. (Revisit "The Right Stuff" in Step #2.)

Create what impassions, electrifies and enlivens you. Create what you must create…what only you can create. Commit to that creation with all your heart, and you will never lack the discipline to get it started…and finished.

Ask Yourself These Questions

Explore these questions in your Way of the Fool journal. Don't think about the answers, and don't feel as though you must answer each question individually if that doesn't feel right. It's okay to find your own way.

Let all your answers (or whatever single answer these questions trigger) emerge freely and honestly, writing them on the Muse Stream in a free-flowing, stream-of-consciousness way where appropriate:

- How do I define discipline? How does that definition feel as I apply it to my creativity?

- How would the time spent with my creative project feel if my discipline were less hard and more heart?

- How can I foster the trust that would free me from hard, unyielding discipline and let my passion propel me forward? What can I do today, now, to foster that trust?

- How passionate am I about this creative project I'm contemplating or working on? How can I nurture and feed that passion? How can I more fully express and experience my commitment — to my creativity and to myself as the creator I am?

Exploration III • Set Yourself Up for Success

Whenever I take on new coaching, consulting or mentoring clients, I always end our first session by asking, "How much time can you realistically devote to your creative project over the next week?" Whatever the answer, I nearly always insist they cut it in half.

It's human nature to set overambitious goals. It's also what we're taught in school and what we're encouraged to do by most coaches, books, seminars and workshops and by most success programs.

Unfortunately, it's also human nature to judge ourselves harshly when we don't achieve those goals.

At best, when we miss our target, we hold to the original goal and try again. At worst, we lower our expectations. In neither case do we feel good about what we have accomplished. In both cases, we mourn our inadequacy rather than celebrating whatever it was we managed to create.

Isn't it better to set a goal that's easily achievable and reach it, rather than set a super-ambitious one and miss the mark? Isn't it better to set a goal of twenty minutes a day and meet that goal, rather than one or two hours a day and end up working on your project for only twenty minutes?

You may ask: "If the result is the same under both scenarios, what difference does it make?" The difference is how we feel about what we have accomplished…or failed to accomplish.

In the first situation, we feel sensational — about ourselves and about our creativity. We feel as though we have succeeded. In the second, we feel discouraged, and our perceived failure could continue to haunt and disable us as we move forward.

Or here's a worse case: You set that two-hours-a-day goal, then abandon it because you can't find those two hours. You might have found twenty minutes, but that wasn't your goal, so you get nothing done that day.

That's why I urge you to set yourself up for success not for failure by giving yourself ridiculously easy goals and meeting them, easily. If that means committing to ten minutes a week of creative work, that's fine. Set your goal and meet it. Then build on that success by gradually increasing your goal.

It's important to build up a sense of the possible, to continue proving to yourself that you can do it. Applying unrealistic goals that you fail to meet underlines your challenges and fuels disappointment and discouragement. Instead, let each success breed more confidence and each confidence, more success.

Set yourself up for success, and before you know it, you will have finished this project and will already be eager to start on the next!

Oh, and don't forget to celebrate each success. That's what Step #12 is all about.

Try This

Have you set yourself an overambitious goal for your creative project, a goal you're challenged to meet? It could be a productivity goal; it could be a time goal. Whichever it is, cut it by half or more, enough that you can achieve it *easily*. As you meet your new goal, find a meaningful way to honor yourself for your success. See Step #12 for suggestions. Then increase your goal bit by bit, either from one day to the next or one week to the next.

Creating on the Muse Stream

Now that you have adopted a healthier approach to goals, discipline and success, revisit "Creating on the Muse Stream" from Step #1, and repeat the exercise.

When You're Finished...

How was this creative session different from others you have experienced? In process? In content? In emotional response? In resistance? Take a few minutes and note those differences, along with how the experience made you feel, in your Way of the Fool journal.

The Way of the Writing Fool

Madeleine L'Engle received two years' worth of rejections from twenty-six publishers (including her own) for the young adult classic *A Wrinkle in Time.*

Toward the end of that demoralizing period, L'Engle covered her typewriter and decided to quit — not only *A Wrinkle in Time* but writing.

Her resolution was short-lived. On her way from typewriter to kitchen, inspiration struck: an idea for a novel about failure. In a flash, she was back at the typewriter.

"That night," she explained three decades later in a PBS documentary, "I wrote in my journal, 'I'm a writer. That's who I am. That's what I am. That's what I have to do — even if I'm never, ever published again.' And I had to take seriously the fact that I might never, ever be published again."

Of course, Madeleine L'Engle was published again: Farrar, Straus and Giroux picked up *A Wrinkle in Time* in 1962.

The following year, *Wrinkle* won the coveted Newbery Medal for children's literature, and by 1989 L'Engle had added four equally popular sequels to what then became *The Time Quintet*. In the decades since, *Wrinkle* has been translated into more than fifteen languages and adapted for the stage multiple times.

"It's easy to say I'm a writer now," L'Engle added, "but I said it when it was hard to say. And I meant it."

My Story: Coda

There would be many more next steps on my writerly journey in the years that followed my resignation from my PR job. I took the most recent while working on this book.

I had registered for an online "boot camp" designed to help me develop strategies for promoting my writing groups and workshops: three full days of nonstop motivation, inspiration, planning and practical exercises. Even our lunch breaks weren't breaks at all; there was always a speaker to keep us engaged while we ate.

The material was powerful, and much of it aligned with the principles I have long written about and taught.

Maybe that was the problem, because halfway through the second afternoon, in a visioning exercise I could easily have devised, my inner vision revealed that I was in the wrong place.

"Close your eyes," the facilitator said, "and imagine yourself a year from now, living your passion. What do you see?"

All the other participants saw themselves successfully offering the kinds of events and programs for which the boot camp was preparing us. Not me.

The instant I closed my eyes, I saw myself sitting at a book-signing table. The queue of readers waiting for me stretched deep into the bookstore. And the stacks of books next to me were flying off the table…only to be replaced by fresh stacks, which disappeared as quickly.

Nothing about my vision had anything to do with the event's primary focus.

"I love to teach," I said to myself that evening as I thought back to the exercise, "and I love to work with writers, especially those struggling to get their stories out. But is it my primary passion? Is it my highest vision for myself?"

NO!

I didn't shout the answer, but I might as well have because I felt it throughout my body.

"I'm a storyteller," I then heard myself say out loud, echoing Madeleine L'Engle. "That's who I am. That's what I am. The author, the writer, the screenwriter, the speaker — they're all expressions of the storyteller I am. That's my primary passion. That's my highest vision for myself. That has always been the most important thing in my life, even when I wasn't consciously aware of it. It still is."

In that moment, I realized that while I had spent the previous year trying to inspire my students and clients to commit more fully to their passion for writing, I hadn't walked the talk.

Now, I would. Now, I would recommit to the writer I am, to the storyteller I am. I would commit to finishing *The Way of the Creative Fool*, which I'd been working on, off and on, for over a year. I would commit to finishing the fifth *Q'ntana* book, *The Lost Horse of Bryn Doon*, which I had been working on for nearly four years. I would commit to completing my three memoirs-in-progress, one of which, ironically titled *All That Matters Is That I'm Writing*, had been dogging me for more than a decade.

Moreover, I would commit to finding new ways to share my stories, including starting a podcast.[1]

I would commit to my passion.

---

[1] The podcast, *Stories & Reflections*, is live at www.storiesandreflections.com.

Declaration

I, *your full name*, commit fully and Fool-ly to my passion for creative expression. I demonstrate that commitment starting today by setting reasonable, achievable goals and by meeting or exceeding those goals. And so it is.

Step #11. Reject Rejection

*Don't ever give up on your art,
and your art will never give up on you.*
THE EMMELINE PAPERS, THE SARA STORIES, BOOK 3

Creative artists are rebels.
Creative artists are renegades.
Creative artists are way showers.

Creative artists defy tradition, flout convention and smash through every status quo they encounter.

Creative artists break with the past,
ignore the present and
cast their gaze toward a future only they can imagine.

Such radical leaps of vision inevitably open them to judgment, mockery and ridicule.

To rejection.

However callous the judgment,
however humiliating the mockery,
however cruel the ridicule,
creative artists persist and persevere.

However demoralizing the rejection,
creative artists manage, somehow,
to transcend it...
to keep going...
to keep creating.

My Story

It's April 1998. Since February, I have been living in a shared house on Pauline Avenue in Toronto's Portuguese neighborhood, a situation I'd found a month earlier when I answered an ad in *Now*, the city's alternative weekly.

We're six, two women and three other guys — all strangers to me when I arrived.

Our first months together were warm, amicable and, if not familial, certainly cooperative. Upon moving in, we'd each committed to a communal meal once a week and to maintaining a vegetarian kitchen, an arrangement that quickly turned strangers into friends and dissolved my initial anxiety about living in this kind of house-share.

Now, though, I need to get the hell out.

Ray has declared that the vegetarian house rule is bullshit. Same goes for the weekly communal meal. As far as he's concerned, he's renting a room. Period. We can do whatever the hell we want; he will no longer participate.

Nor will he move out. Not initially, when the rest of us remind him of the commitment he made when he was vetted. Not a few weeks later when he and Roger get into a fistfight so intense that the police are called and we ask them both to leave.

As our "community" self-destructs over the next weeks. I realize I can't stay, and I give a month's notice.

I'm not concerned about finding a new place. Even with

Roxy, my two-year-old cocker spaniel, how hard can it be to find a suitable rental? This is Toronto, after all, with a metro population of 4.4 million. There have to be thousands upon thousands of possibilities.

Harder, as it turns out, than I would have thought.

Rental after rental rejects me because of Roxy, and by month's end I give up. I will stay on Pauline Avenue and live with the friction and unpleasantness.

"No you won't," reply my fellow housemates — sans Ray, who's around but doesn't care, and Roger, who has decamped.

While I have been home-hunting, Roger's room has been rented to a young woman who is allergic to dogs; the Pauline Avenue house is going pet-free.

Roxy and I are out.

The rejections don't end there.

I store my few belongings in the healing/writing studio I'm renting and leave town for a week's camping in MacGregor Point Provincial Park, hoping its rocks, pines and Lake Huron waters will offer me some direction.

They don't, at least not until I'm back in the city, when I feel guided to book into a hotel around the corner from my first Toronto apartment. It feels odd wandering around my old neighborhood. Foreign. Like a farewell…not that I understand what I'm leaving behind.

Not yet.

My second night, that same inner voice sends me, inexplicably, to Richmond Hill, a bedroom community north of the city. Despite my doubts, I follow the flow of commuter traffic out of Toronto. And when I reach the town's old main street, I start looking for motels.

"Sorry," the first desk clerk says. "No dogs."

Next motel, same rejection.

I curse silently. "If the next motel rejects us," I grumble

to Roxy, "we're going back to Toronto and the Town Inn. I don't care what my guidance says."

A few blocks up the road from that second motel is another, clean but nondescript.

"A dog?" The front desk clerk peers over his glasses at me, then down at Roxy.

I clench my teeth, waiting for the inevitable rebuff. *Town Inn, here I come.*

"How many nights?"

"Just the one."

He studies Roxy.

"Just one night, you say?" he asks after a long pause.

I nod.

He pulls a key from the rack.

"Follow me." He marches across the parking lot. "Just for one night," he calls back over his shoulder.

I'm grateful but angry. And scared. How many more nights can I live like this?

A night's sleep fails to calm me. If anything, I'm more anxious as I face a new day. I have a few hours before checkout, so I take Roxy for a walk. At the edge of the property, I discover a wooded trail that drops into an overgrown ravine. I slip off my Birkenstocks, free Roxy from her leash and start down.

As we reach the bottom, it's as though a lightbulb flicks on over my head, like in those old comic strips. I know what I am to do. I will book into a hotel for the next several days and use that time to wind down my Toronto life. When that's done, Roxy and I will get in the car with whatever is left and take a leap of faith onto the Way of the Fool.

A week later, we're again heading north out of the city; this time, on the Trans-Canada Highway…destination unknown.

Three months and fourteen thousand meandering

miles later, the Way of the Fool lands me in Sedona. I assume it's another whistle-stop on the way to wherever, not yet aware that *this* is my "wherever" and that all those Toronto and Richmond Hill rejections served a deeper purpose. They were setting me up for a new life I could never have imagined, in a new country I would never have expected to call home.

The Way of the Fool

The Fool takes no notice of others' criticisms. The Fool is unmoved by others' judgments. The Fool is untroubled by others' rejections. Nor do others' praise or plaudits influence her words or actions.

He takes no account of others' views of his best efforts, dismissing them as extraneous and irrelevant. To her, such views inevitably reveal more about the judge than they do about the judged.

In all he is and all he does, the Fool is guided by his heart alone. That infinite and eternal wisdom is all the counsel she needs…or heeds.

Your Story

Exploration I • Embracing the "All" of You

There's a scene in TV's *Star Trek: The Next Generation* where Jean-Luc Picard is presented with a sculpture of a humanoid. When he lifts the piece's removable top, more than a dozen identical beings are nested inside. Like that sculpture, we carry within us many facets and aspects that make up the greater whole we view as Self.

If you're feeling hypercritical about some aspect of your creativity, it can be helpful to identify and connect with the part of you that is trapped in self-judgment.

How? It's not as hard as it might sound. First, let me tell you a story…

Some years back, I woke up nauseous and sweating from a nightmare. In the dream, I was trying to walk out of a multilevel parking structure, but the uniformed attendant refused to let me pass. I argued. He argued back. I shouted. He shouted back. Whatever I said or did was met with unyielding resistance.

A few days later, in an experience similar to the one I describe in Step #7's "My Story," I decided to reproduce the dream in meditation to see if I could alter the outcome. I called the surly guard back into my consciousness and he again blocked me from leaving. This time, instead of arguing, I calmly asked him why. Over the course of our conversation, he revealed that his job was to protect me.

"If I let you leave here," he said, "I will be out of work."

At first, I was startled by the disclosure. Then, from some deep well of inner wisdom, I reassured him that I continued to need his protection, but in new ways.

With that, he agreed to learn to act more as a filter than a block, we embraced, and I strode past him and out into the sunlight, having turned an obstacle into an eager helper.

Now it's your turn…

Meditation: Taming Your Inner Critic

Have your Way of the Fool journal handy to record your thoughts, feelings and impressions. Allow at least 30 minutes for this experience, longer if you plan further explorations in your journal once you have completed the meditation.

My studio recording of "Taming Your Inner Critic," one nearly identical to this version, is available for download or streaming[1] as part of "The Voice of the Muse Companion: Guided Meditations for Writers."

Revisit "Getting Started" to find out how to access the recording, as well as for tips on how best to use this book's meditations, visualizations and meditative journeys.

Sit or lie down in a comfortable position. Close your eyes and take a few deep breaths. Let yourself relax. Feel yourself relax on your breath.

Now, let your shoulders drop…and drop some more. And some more. And some more.

Breathe deeply and fully, feeling the breath fill not only your lungs and abdomen but your entire body — from head to toes and back again.

And again.

And again.

Feel the breath cleanse you. Feel it dissolve your fears,

---

[1] Search the relevant site/store for "Mark David Gerson inner critic."

your anxiety, your stress. Feel it strengthen you, empower you. Feel it protect you, keep you safe. Feel it open your heart. Feel it open your mind. There have been times in your life when you have been criticized, times in your life when you have been judged. Of course there have. We have all had those experiences. As children. As adolescents. As adults.

Sometimes, the experience rolled off us painlessly. Sometimes, it felt excruciatingly cruel. Sometimes, we forged ahead in spite of it. Sometimes, it shut us down.

It's all normal, all perfect, all part of the human experience. And as with all human experience, we can choose how to react or respond, we can choose how each instance will affect us.

Don't judge how you have reacted or responded in the past. Simply be aware and keep breathing. Fully. Deeply. Allow your breath to once again dissolve any stress or anxiety triggered by unpleasant memories.

Know you are safe.

Protected.

Free from harm of any sort.

From that place of relaxed breathing, from that place of safety, call into your mind, heart and/or consciousness your harshest critic.

Perhaps it's someone in your past or present life. A parent. A sibling. Another relative. A current or former boyfriend, girlfriend or life partner. A teacher. A friend. A school or neighborhood bully. A boss, professional colleague or coworker. Anyone, whoever it is.

Feel whatever charge you feel around this individual, and breathe. Feel whatever charge you feel around this individual and let that feeling dissolve on your breath.

Now, let that critic transform into some kind of image, something that represents that critic, that stands in for that critic. A symbol. A metaphor. Perhaps it's an animal.

Perhaps it's a color or shape. Perhaps it's a snake or monster. Perhaps it's another human form or another type of form altogether. Or perhaps it doesn't change form at all.

Let it be what it is and know that however it shows up is perfect for you in this moment. Regardless of how it shows up, see it not as an external critic but as an internalized aspect of you, ready to engage with you.

Whatever it is, whoever it is, however it is, greet it and begin a dialogue with it. Have a conversation with it.

Engage with it.

Either write this dialogue as it occurs, or let it emerge silently in your heart.

In the first part of your conversation, ask your critic why it judged you so cruelly, what provoked its behavior, what it was afraid of. If this is an ongoing situation, frame your questions in the present tense.

Listen with an open heart. Respond with an open heart. Allow compassion. Allow understanding. Allow forgiveness. Allow love.

Give yourself thirty seconds of clock time for this part of the experience. Or pause the meditation until you are ready to continue.

Be aware that if you are experiencing judgment, there are probably areas in your life where you are expressing judgment. Have compassion for yourself for your judgments. Be understanding. Be forgiving. Be loving. Be open. Be respectful. Toward yourself.

Commit as well to directing those same attitudes toward others, toward anyone you are tempted to criticize harshly.

Now, as you return to the conversation with your critic, ask it how the two of you can work together moving forward to bring your work, your creativity and your life to its fullest, most magnificent potential.

Converse. Discuss. Negotiate. Dialogue. Engage. Silently or in writing.

Again, be loving and compassionate. Be understanding and forgiving. Be respectful. Be open.

Allow another thirty seconds of clock time for this part of the experience. Or, again, pause the meditation until you're ready to continue.

Now it's time to bring your encounter to a close. Thank this aspect of yourself for its assistance, for its openness, for its willingness to transform. And commit to this new partnership. Commit, too, to the spirit of cooperation the two of you have just forged in love and mutual respect.

When you're done, write of your experiences and discoveries in your Way of the Fool journal. Use all your senses to paint a picture in words of your new awareness and your renewed creative power. Or express the experience in another creative medium. Whatever works for you is perfect.

When you're finished, remember to read your words or revisit your creation from a place of love, openness and nonjudgment. Remember, too, your commitment to partnership and cooperation.

Exploration II • The Road to Empowerment

Most creative artists don't work in a vacuum. Whether it's a book we hope others will read, a piece of music we hope others will hear, a play, film, photograph, painting, drawing or sculpture we hope others will see, a recipe we hope others will taste or a garden we yearn to show off, most of us create at least as much for an audience as for ourselves.

As creative artists, there is a time to hold your work to yourself and a time to share it out into the world. Only you can know which time is which. Only you can discern how, when and with whom to begin the process.

Feedback can be part of that process. It involves selectively sharing your creation in order to receive what will help you strengthen your work and support you in your creativity. Selectively, because not everyone is equipped to supply you with what you require, nor is everyone able to support you in the ways you need, desire and deserve.

Notice that I avoid words like "criticism" and "critique." For many, these words hold an emotional charge of harshness and negativity, even of cruelty. Words, as Alice discovered in Wonderland, bear the meanings we ascribe to them far more than they do their strict dictionary definitions. To me, "feedback" carries with it the potential for a more positive, supportive response than does "criticism" or "critique."

Ultimately, however, the tone and tenor of any solicited response to your work is up to you. Are you seeking "sympathetic vibrations," one of the synonyms for "feedback" you'll find in *Roget's International Thesaurus*, or are you opening yourself to that other, less supportive definition, "unwanted noise"? It's that second type of feedback that can too easily trigger creative blocks and shutdowns.

This is your work, your creative process. You have the right and the obligation to choose when you will seek feedback and from whom. You also have the right and obligation to select the precise nature and level of feedback you will receive. You cannot control your creative journey, but you can empower yourself in it.

How do you ensure that others' views and comments support your creation, not distort it? By always following my "Seven Be's of Empowered Feedback" whenever you share your creative work with anyone, including your best friend, your parents, a fellow artist or your life partner.

Seven Be's of Empowered Feedback

1. Be Protective

Your work is as much your creation as is your child. You have no more right to knowingly expose it to influences that could harm it or set it back than you do your child.

Seek out only those people who will support you and your work. Never assume that those closest to you will fall into that category. Often, without meaning to hurt you, they are the most critical and least helpful.

When someone asks to experience your work-in-progress or preview your finished work, always use your discernment when considering the request, and give yourself permission to say no, when appropriate. This applies equally to fellow artists as well as to feedback circles or critique groups.

Get a sense of any creative peer group before joining and, once you are attending, note the type of feedback offered by its members before agreeing to share your work.

The sole reason to offer feedback is to support the creator and his or her work. Not all groups share that philosophy.

- *See "A Community of Creative Fools," later in the book, for tips on setting up your own group.*

2. Be Open

Your work, like your child, requires fresh air and outside influences. Don't let fear make you overprotective and hold you back from sharing your work and your vision. Be open to others' perceptions, comments and responses.

At the same time, exercise discernment in determining which of those are relevant and which can be dismissed at this moment in your work's development and your own.

3. Be Aware

To everything there is a season. At different stages in your creative process, you will be ready to hear different things from different people. Respect where you are and seek only the type and depth of feedback you are prepared to receive, integrate and apply. Recognize when you are at your most raw and respect that too. As always, discernment is key.

4. Be Clear

Be clear within yourself about the type of feedback you require and desire at this stage on your journey with your work. For example, are you seeking highly detailed input? Or do you prefer general comments? Or do you want nothing more than a pat on the back for having completed a first draft, an early sketch, a particularly challenging part of the project…or simply for having started?

Only you can determine what will support your creative process at this time and what might damage it, so…

5. Be Explicit

Once you have discerned the type and depth of feedback that is appropriate for you and your work at this time, ask for it — directly, unambiguously and with neither apology nor equivocation. Others cannot know how best to support you unless you make your needs clear. Don't be shy or embarrassed to make those needs known. If you are vague, hesitant or equivocal, you open yourself to comments that you may not be ready to hear, comments that could feel hurtful or damaging, even if they are not intended to be so.

6. Be Strong

Know what you want, and don't be afraid to speak up

— clearly, lovingly, compassionately and, again, without apology — when you are not getting it, or when you are getting something you didn't ask for. This is your work, your project, your creative journey. It's up to you to identify what will help and support you as you birth it and bring it to completion. In this, you are not only training yourself to seek out what will assist you, you are training others to provide feedback in supportive ways and to seek it for themselves in empowered ways.

7. Be Discerning

Your creative output is an expression of you, yet it is not you. Negative comments, whether deliberately cruel or not, have no power to harm you unless you abdicate your power and allow yourself to be hurt. Deep inside, you know your work's strengths and weaknesses. Tap into that intuitive knowingness and rely on it to discern which comments it is wisest to ignore and which support you and serve your creative project.

Seeking Feedback? Ask Yourself These Questions...

- How can I be clearer within myself about the feedback I need and with others about the feedback I am seeking?

- How can I be more discerning about to whom I turn for feedback?

- Where have I been burnt in the past when seeking feedback? How can I avoid that in the future?

- How can I be more respectful of my work's needs and my own when seeking feedback?

- How can I be more discriminating in determining which feedback to take to heart and which to dismiss?

- Do I apply the "Seven Be's" when others ask me for feedback? If not, can I commit to respecting others' work and creative process in the same way I seek to have my work and process respected?

Six Tips for Rising Above Rejection

Rare is the creative artist who never experiences rejection. Has an agent, publisher, producer, gallery owner, competition judge or other decision maker passed on your work? Has a critic scarred you with a devastating review? Has a life partner, parent, child, sibling, friend, neighbor or stranger judged your work harshly? It doesn't matter whether the censure is intentionally cruel. It still stings. When that happens, here are six ways to ease you through and past the pain.

1. Real Men Cry; Real Women Cry Too

Don't bottle up your feelings. Don't get self-destructive. Feel what you feel. Feel all of it. Cry. Curse. Yell. Scream. Throw things. Throw up. Then get past the rejection and move on.

2. Inject Your Feelings into Your Creations

Powerful emotions birth powerful creative expression. Writing fiction, a screenplay or a stage play? Channel your emotions into a character — if not as part of a current project, then as part of another. Creating visual art? Hurl your bitterness onto your canvas, render it onto your sketch pad or gouge it into wood, stone or clay. Working in another form, medium or genre? Find your own perfect release. None of the preceding outlets is practical? Spew your humiliation, disappointment, resentment, anger, frustration, pain and despair onto the pages of your Way of the Fool journal.

3. Take Creator's Revenge
Subject whoever rejected you to something unspeakably hideous and horrific…in writing, or on your canvas or sketch pad. In the kitchen? What ingredient can you chop, dice, shred, mash or smash that can stand in for the insensitive culprit? Whatever your medium and however you manage it, find the creator's equivalent of sticking pins into a voodoo doll. Whatever you create (or destroy) is unlikely to make it into any of your finished work, but you will have more fun with it than you ought to admit.

4. Look for the Silver Lining
Every experience, however emotionally debilitating, contains within it the seeds of something positive. You may not be able to see the redemptive value of this rebuff or criticism today, or even tomorrow. And that's fine. But once the pain has begun to subside, be open to a flash of insight that will reveal the silver lining around your storm cloud of rejection.

5. Look for the Spark of Truth
It doesn't happen often, but your rejection letter could include reasons for the turndown, apart from the standard "does not meet our needs at this time." Or the critic could offer constructive suggestions. If someone has taken the effort to offer feedback, pay attention to it. Use the discernment mentioned in "The Seven Be's of Empowered Feedback" to determine if the comments highlight real weaknesses that it would serve you to address — in a revision or in new work.

6. Don't Give Up!

Don't let one rejection, criticism or terrible review — or a hundred or a thousand — stop you. Keep creating and keep seeking ways to become a better artist.

Ask Yourself These Questions

Explore these questions in your Way of the Fool journal. Don't think about the answers, and don't feel as though you must answer each question individually if that doesn't feel right. It's okay to find your own way.

Let all your answers (or whatever single answer these questions trigger) emerge freely and honestly, writing them on the Muse Stream in a free-flowing, stream-of-consciousness way where appropriate:

- How have I handled rejection or harsh criticism in unhealthy ways in the past?

- How can I handle my next disappointment or rejection in a more healthy, productive way than I did the last one?

- Can I refuse to let criticism or rejection stop me from moving forward with this or with any other of my creative projects?

- If I am unable to find representation or if my work isn't selling or attracting an audience, can I trust that there may be other reasons why I was called to create it? Can I be okay with that?

Creating on the Muse Stream

Now that you have given up on giving up and have engaged

with your inner critic and reassessed your relationship with rejection, revisit "Creating on the Muse Stream" from Step #1, and repeat the exercise.

When You're Finished…

How was this creative session different from others you have experienced? In process? In content? In emotional response? In resistance? Take a few minutes and note those differences, along with how the experience made you feel, in your Way of the Fool journal.

The Way of Six Cinematic Fools

1. The Exorcist (1973)

Hollywood initially wanted nothing to do with *The Exorcist*. It probably didn't help that the book wasn't selling well. Then, in one of those plot twists that happens only in the movies, author/screenwriter William Peter Blatty scored a last-minute appearance on *The Dick Cavett Show* when a scheduled guest dropped out, and his spot was extended thanks to another guest's drinking problem. The resulting spike in book sales caused Warner Bros. to reconsider its initial turndown. Now ranked as one of the most influential horror films of all time, *The Exorcist* earned ten Oscar nominations, including one for Blatty's screenplay.

2. Star Wars (1977)

No one wanted the first *Star Wars* film. United Artists, Universal, Paramount and (ironically) Disney all passed on it. Although Twentieth Century Fox said yes, it didn't expect much from it, consigning the film to a limited release. The rest (not to mention eleven Oscars, eleven more films to date, and a series franchise said to be worth more than $65 *billion*) is history. Where's the irony? In 2012 Disney paid $4.05 billion for Lucasfilm in a deal that included all existing *Star Wars* movies, characters and related intellectual property.

3. Raiders of the Lost Ark (1981)

Dropping Steven Spielberg into the director's chair didn't initially help *Raiders of the Lost Ark*, which most studios rejected, considering it too expensive for a film with no big-name stars attached. *Raiders of the Lost Ark* won five of its nine Oscar nominations and is now considered to be among the best action-adventure films of all time.

4. E.T. the Extra-Terrestrial (1982)

Columbia Pictures might still be kicking itself for throwing *E.T.* under the bike…after it had already spent a million dollars on it in development. At the time, though, even the Spielberg name wasn't enough for studio decision makers, who called it a "wimpy Walt Disney movie." Spielberg took the project to Universal, where *E.T.* would grab four Oscars and become the highest-grossing movie ever at the time.

5. Back to the Future (1985)

It took some forty-four studio rejections before Universal said yes to *Back to the Future*. Other studios had complained that it was either "too family friendly" or "not family-friendly enough." Disney was alarmed by allusions to mother-son incest, while Columbia felt it was "not sexual enough." Nominated for more than two dozen awards, including four Oscars (it won one) and four Golden Globes, *Back to the Future* was the top-grossing film of 1985.

6. Dirty Dancing (1987)

Dirty Dancing had nearly as many turndowns as *Back to the Future:* forty ("too small," "too soft" and "too girly"). Even then, it took a radical budget cut to get it into production. Ultimately, Vestron's $5 million investment paid off…nearly fifty-fold. And the movie's signature song, "(I've Had) The Time of My Life," won the Oscar for Best Original Song.

My Story: Coda

I would take off on a half-dozen similar, Fool-like journeys over the next twenty-five years, odysseys that carried me not only from coast to coast and back into Canada but across the Pacific to Hawaii. Each one launched me into an unexpected new life I could never have imagined for myself, all triggered by those long ago Toronto rejections.

Declaration

I, *your name*, acknowledge and affirm that I am undaunted by others' judgments and undeterred by others' rejections. In all I am, all I do and all I create, I walk the Way of the Creative Fool, guided solely by the voice of my Muse and the spirit of my deepest essence. And so it is.

Step #12. Celebrate Your Creations...and Your Creativity

Don't do "half-empty glass" on yourself.
Your glass is more than half full. Notice that.
Acknowledge that. Celebrate that.
Dialogues with the Divine:
Encounters with My Wisest Self

Why mourn what you have not yet created?
Why focus on what you have not yet completed?
Why sacrifice a single breath on
the as yet untraveled miles ahead?

Celebrate instead the great distance
you have already traveled...
the miles you have already journeyed.

Celebrate instead
all you have already accomplished,
all you have already achieved,
all you have already created.

Celebrate your individuality.

Celebrate your originality.
Celebrate your creativity.

Celebrate you.

My Story

MANY MOCKED SALLY FIELD in 1979 when she exclaimed, during her Oscar speech for her *Norma Rae* best-actress win, "You like me. You really like me!" I have experienced countless Sally Field moments of my own over the years. Perhaps the most dramatic occurred in 2011 when the independent producer committed to film adaptations of my *Legend of Q'ntana* fantasy novels arranged to shoot a series of promotional trailers to help raise funds for the project.

I wrote a short script for each of what, then, were the series' three stories, and we filmed them over two February weekends with the help of a volunteer cast and crew, all professionals.

As we set up on our makeshift soundstage that first weekend, it was hard for me to conceive that everyone present was there because of me…because of my words and my vision.

For large chunks of those four twelve-hour days, my mind struggled to accept that fact. I would hear my dialogue spoken by costumed, in-character actors and not be able to connect the experience with the words I had penned and the scenes I had envisioned.

In part, that was a good thing. It afforded me an ego-free objectivity that allowed me to see what worked and what didn't. Often, though, it felt like I was strangely not present, even though my physical body was consuming large quantities of sweetened coffee to keep me functioning after a week's anxious sleeplessness — the same wake-me-up that had kept me going through another birth eleven years earlier: my daughter's.

There were flashes, of course...moments when I did recognize that I had written what I was seeing and hearing. Those moments were indescribable validations of the power of my dreams and imagination, a power that I realized I couldn't fully trust or acknowledge...let alone celebrate. I had experienced similar moments during our casting calls and rehearsals, when actors proved to my doubting mind that my dialogue worked and my stories were sound. I even cried during particularly powerful readings. Now, with recreations of my characters interacting in recreations of my worlds, the proof was incontrovertible.

I was gratified, stunned...and scared. Like a Sally Field surprised by the depth of her gifts, I didn't know what to do with that proof. And like a Sally Field startled by the praise of her peers, I didn't know what to say when, at the close of each shooting day, actors thanked me for my stories and for the privilege of playing my characters.

Just as I had wept when I'd held an advance copy of the published *MoonQuest* book in 2007, so I wept when the second assistant camera operator clicked her slate in front of the camera and called out, "Scene 10, Take 1. Marker." It was Saturday morning, the first take of the first scene to be shot...still among most powerful and validating moments of my creative life...and still a moment worth celebrating.

The Way of the Fool

The Fool sees no need to distinguish between large accomplishments and small ones, nor between success and failure. The Fool celebrates it all.

Life itself is a celebration to the Fool. There is nothing in his life that is not worthy of grateful acknowledgment… nothing in her life that does not merit rejoicing.

Each step is a gift.

Each moment is a blessing.

Each breath is a benediction.

The Fool knows that when you celebrate life as it shows up, however it shows up, life celebrates you in return.

Celebration: That is the Way of the Fool.

Your Story

Meditation: Celebrate Your Creative Power

Have your Way of the Fool journal handy to record your thoughts, feelings and impressions. Allow at least 30 minutes for this experience, longer if you plan further explorations in your journal once you have completed the meditation.

Revisit "Getting Started" for more tips on how best to use this book's meditations, visualizations and meditative journeys.

Close your eyes. Relax. Get comfortable.

Take a deep breath in, then let it go. Another…then let that one go. And another…then let that one go.

Let your shoulders drop. Feel the tension drain from your shoulders…from your neck…from your arms. From every part of your body — head to toes and toes to head.

If you're sitting, let your hands fall to your lap. If you're lying down, let them fall to your abdomen.

And continue to focus on your breath. In…and out. In…and out. In…and out.

Was there anything about your day that was harsh or jarring? Words, perhaps? Actions? Thoughts, even? They could have been yours, directed at yourself or another. Or they could have been someone else's, directed at you or another. Whatever and whichever, let them go on your next series of exhalations.

All of them.

Breathe in peace and calm. And breathe out another aspect of your day that isn't in alignment with your highest essence — your highest creative essence but also your highest life essence.

Take a moment or two to repeat that.

Breathe in peace and calm.

Breathe out anything that is not peace and calm. Anything. From anyone. From anywhere.

And any moment that was particularly wonderful, breathe that in, deeply. Reconnect with the energy of that.

Now, again, breathe out any aspect of your day or life that was not wonderful, that was not peace and calm.

If you need to do more than breathe it out, blow it out. Take the deepest breath you can, then blow out all the day's detritus…all the day's incoherence…all the day's jangle… all the day's grating people and jarring experiences. Blow them out. As fully and noisily as you dare. More noisily than you dare.

Blow them out until they're gone. Gone from your mind. Gone from your awareness. Gone from your body. Gone. Vanished, as though they never existed.

Now that you're clear and fully invested in this moment, breathe in to your power…your creative power… your creative essence.

Breathe into it fully. Deeply. Completely.

Your creative power. Your creative essence.

Wherever you are on your creative journey — whatever stage you're at, however long you've been at it — this is a power and essence you have yet to fully acknowledge and embrace. A power and essence you have yet to celebrate.

For how can you celebrate it if you don't first acknowledge it? If you can't first acknowledge it?

So acknowledge it.

Whether you have been creating for five minutes, five

days, five months or five years, the journey you traveled to that first moment of creative awareness, that first moment when you sensed a call to express yourself in an original way, was a long one…longer than your conscious mind can measure. For, like the seeds planted in the soil that germinate and grow in the invisible realm beneath the earth's surface, your call to create also had its origins in the unseen, the unknown, the unknowable.

Then, once you heard the call, there is likely to have been another journey before you felt able to answer it. And you did feel able to answer it, at least in some way, or you wouldn't be here right now…couldn't be here right now.

From that first call and answer, there have been other calls. Calls you answered and calls you chose to ignore. The calls you answered brought you to this time, to this place. Even the calls you ignored ultimately brought you here.

To this moment of acknowledgment.

To this moment of celebration. Joyous celebration.

Yes, *joyous* celebration.

Celebration of your voice, however it expresses itself. Of your creative essence, however it expresses itself. Of your creative power, however it expresses itself.

They have all expressed themselves, in some way. For if you have made it this far on the Way of the Creative Fool, then you are already creating.

And what you're creating is good enough. Of course, it's good enough because you created it, and you are good enough. You are more than good enough. You are an expression of the divine in human form. How, then, can you not be good enough?

So take a moment and breathe that in. The power of your voice, however it expresses itself. The power of your creative essence, however it expresses itself. The essence of your creative power, however it expresses itself.

Acknowledge it. Trust that it's true. And celebrate it. In your heart, of course. But also in your mind.

You doubt me? How can you when you have already created what no one else ever could because what you created is as an expression of your unique heart, of your singular journey and, yes, of your extraordinary gifts?

So take a moment and breathe that in. Acknowledge it. Trust that it's true. And celebrate it. In your heart, of course. But also in your mind.

Now cast your mind back in time. Cast your mind to the beginnings of your conscious creative journey. As you do, note the highlights of that journey. The low-lights, too, that you transcended. The setbacks you experienced that didn't stop you from continuing the journey that has brought you to this day.

And, of course, the successes. The triumphs. The victories. The accomplishments. The achievements. Breathe deeply into all of those as you acknowledge each. And as you acknowledge each, celebrate it. For each success, however minor it might seem in retrospect, is worth celebrating.

Whether minor or major, a setback overcome, an easy win or an overnight success that was years in the making, each has been a paving stone on the journey that brought you to this moment on your Creative Fool's odyssey that is, itself, worthy of celebration.

So take a moment and breathe in each of those paving stones. Every one, even if you can't recall when, how or why each was laid. Acknowledge them and breathe them in. Every one. Named or not. For you have traveled a journey of exceptional courage. You have journeyed. You have persevered. You have refused to give in or give up.

Can you see how remarkable an achievement that has been? How remarkable an achievement it is? Whatever you can see of it with your conscious mind, multiply that awareness by a hundred. By a thousand. By a million. By hundred thousand million. By the number of stars in the entirety of the cosmos. For in a world where so many refuse their creative power, or acknowledge it only to give up, you are part of the tiniest of minorities. The bravest of minorities. The mightiest of minorities.

So acknowledge and celebrate that.

You have so much to celebrate. So much. And all those celebrations are of you.

Yes, of you.

So take another moment and do more than acknowledge all you are and all you have traveled to reach this moment on your creative journey. Celebrate it. Celebrate you.

Don't limit your celebration to this meditative moment. Commit to acknowledging all your achievements, all your accomplishments and all your successes. And commit to celebrating them. Every one!

Creating on the Muse Stream

Revisit "Creating on the Muse Stream" from Step #1, and repeat the exercise.

When You're Finished…

Now that you have acknowledged the great distances you have already traveled on your creative journey, how was this creative session different from others you have experienced? In process? In content? In emotional response? In resistance? Take a few minutes and note those differences, along with how the experience made you feel, in your Way of the Fool journal. Take a moment, too, to celebrate what you have just created.

Exploration • Your Celebration Diary

Starting tonight, let your final act before lights out be an inventory of your day's successes and accomplishments. Include your creative achievements, of course, but don't limit yourself to them.

Run through them in your mind or catalog them in your Way of the Fool journal. Ignore anything you perceive as a failure, a setback or bad news. Pay no heed to any goal unreached, and disregard any task left undone. Forget recrimination and second-guessing. Don't compare yourself with anyone else, don't compare your work to anyone else's and don't compare today's achievements with yesterday's or last week's. Reject all rejections. (Revisit Step #11 if you continue to be haunted by past rejections.)

Instead, acknowledge everything you achieved and any way in which you did not give up or give in to hopelessness or despair, however inconsequential it might seem to your critical, judgmental mind...or to anyone else. Include any moment when you caught yourself before you plunged into a futile act of pointless comparison.

Include any times when you followed your intuition or took a leap of faith. Creating on the Muse Stream is always a leap of faith.

Include acts of courage. Remember that courage is not synonymous with fearlessness. Courage is your ability to act in spite of fear. Creating from the heart and letting yourself be vulnerable in your artistic expression is always an act of courage.

Include your progress on *The Way of the Creative Fool*.

Include everything. No success is too insignificant to acknowledge.

You have no success to record, you say? I'm not talking

about a publishing contract, a gallery deal, winning an award or signing with an agent or its equivalent in your field. Nor am I talking about a massive creative output, whatever that might look like in your form, medium or genre.

Don't judge what you've produced or how much you've produced. Celebrate that you *have* produced. (You haven't produced anything today? Don't punish yourself. Keep reading.)

Even if what you created won't be seen by anyone but you, it has value. Everything you create has value. Every word that finds its way onto the page, every sketch that finds its way onto your pad, every seed you plant in your garden, every recipe you devise, every project you start (including the ones you never finish)...they all have value.

Did you give *any* energy to your creativity today? To a project-in-progress? To an idea you've been thinking about but haven't yet initiated? Then you have a success to celebrate.

If you didn't focus on your creativity today, don't beat yourself up. Celebrate the time you're spending right now to rekindle the creative spark that brought you to these pages. Reading this chapter counts.

Continue your success inventory for at least ninety days. As you go, notice how your focus evolves from perceived failures and not-good-enoughs toward your real successes and attainments — in your creativity, of course, but also in all aspects of your life. Record that shift in focus, too, in your Way of the Fool journal.

Don't stop there!

Back when I was in public school, teachers would hand out stickers and gold stars when we did well. Why? Because those rewards inevitably fired us up to do even better.

Incentives work. Meaningful incentives work.

What will your gold star be? What's your equivalent

of the schoolroom sticker? How can you celebrate your creative success? What can you do *today* to reward your creative achievements?

Your reward needn't be extravagant or expensive. It could be a specialty coffee at your favorite café, a book you've long coveted, time off for an outing to a favorite place or any acknowledgment that is meaningful to you. Whatever your reward, let it be something special. However you earned it, celebrate it.

That's your reward for today, to get a feel for the power of gold stars…the power of celebration. However, once your success diary has become a daily ritual, reward yourself weekly so that your gold star remains a special treat, not an everyday routine.

Remember to honor yourself, always, for meeting the challenge…whatever it is.

Celebrate your achievements. Energize your accomplishments. Give yourself a gold star. Celebrate you.

The Way of the Literary Fool

"I have written eleven books," Maya Angelou once confessed in an interview, "but each time I think, 'Uh oh, they're going to find me out now. I've run a game on everybody, and they're going to find me out.'"

By the time she died in 2014 at age eighty-six, that book count had nearly tripled, and her writing credits also included screenplays, stage plays and teleplays. And those were merely her literary accomplishments. Maya Angelou was also a Tony- and Emmy-nominated actor and singer, a passionate civil rights activist and the recipient of fifty honorary degrees and dozens of awards.

In other words, Maya Angelou's literary brilliance and other gifts were never in question…except by her. For all she was lauded, applauded and admired, Angelou never fully accepted that her work could be worthy of such acclaim.

Of course, it was and is.

In her own way, Maya Angelou must have believed it… not only for herself, but for all of us. "I believe that each of us comes from the Creator trailing wisps of glory," she said.

And that's something worth celebrating.

My Story: Coda

I still have Sally Field moments. One of the most recent occurred during the closing session of one of my breakthrough mastermind groups…although perhaps I should characterize what happened as an *un*-Sally Field moment.

I had just finished celebrating participants for their vulnerability and courage, for the eloquence of their stories and for how powerfully each had contributed to the success of our time together when one interrupted me.

"None of that could have happened without you and your coaching," she declared.

Instead of pausing, as Sally Field would have done, to acknowledge my student's celebration of me and my work, I ignored her and continued to praise the group.

It was only later that I realized that I had done precisely what I had spent six weeks urging my group *not* to do. I had downplayed their praise and minimized my accomplishments.

That experience would become a teaching moment, and not solely in subsequent groups. It was a teaching moment for me. It still is.

Declaration

I, *your name*, celebrate every aspect of my creative expression and each moment of my creativity. As the Creative

Fool that I am, I honor and rejoice in all my creative accomplishments, achievements and successes, even those my critical mind would dismiss as too minor to acknowledge, recognizing that "energy flows where attention goes." And so it is.

Step #12½. Embrace Your Vision

*In the end, there seemed always but
a single choice: whether or not to
be true to oneself and one's vision.*
THE SUNQUEST, THE LEGEND OF Q'NTANA, BOOK 3

Your vision is the light force of your work,
the life force of your work.
It's the spirit that is its essence,
the breath that keeps it alive.

Your vision is your dream for your work,
the expression of your intention.
It's what guides it, drives it and propels it from
conception to completion...and beyond.
It's what guides, drives and propels you
through every stage of your creative journey with it.

The more deeply you stay connected to that vision,
the more fully your finished project will
remain true to that life force, that dream, that intention.

And the truer you will be to the work
that called upon you to breathe life into it.

My Story

It's late 2008, a week before Christmas. The global economy is crashing, and mine isn't far behind. Three weeks into the one job I have been able to find, as Hobby Lobby's oldest-ever stock boy, I'm feeling desperate and hopeless. The hours are long and physically exhausting, the pay doesn't cover my expenses, and I'm terrified of losing both my car and the condo I'm renting.

I hate my job, and I hate my life.

Friends are sympathetic, but only one offers a suggestion: "Write, write, write," he urges in an email. "It is your soul work. It is your gift."

Sobbing, I read his words over and over. I then recall a promise I made to myself a few months ago: "Regardless of what it takes and what is required of me, I commit to finishing *The StarQuest*. It's time, and I'm ready."

I have two unfinished first drafts of this sequel to *The MoonQuest*, the first dating back more than a decade. Do I try for a *third* first draft? Can I finish a third first draft?

I know it will mean writing every day, something I haven't done since early drafts of *The MoonQuest*. Then, all I had was time. Now…?

Yet I know I have no choice. Telling this story can be the only thing matters…is the only thing that matters.

It is now a few months later and I'm more than two hundred pages into the manuscript, writing a scene that never made it into either of my previous attempts at a first draft.

In the scene, my three protagonists face their most daunting test. As they trek through the spiraling series of caves, caverns and tunnels known as The Coil, each must discover his or her greatest fear then move through it. The sole alternative is madness…or death.

Q'nta, whose son was snatched from her when he was an infant, only to be taken from her again soon after they are reunited many years later, expects her greatest fear to be a permanent separation from Ben. It isn't. To her surprise — as to mine as soon as I write the words — it is the loss of her storytelling gifts.

"How can losing my stories be my nightmare?" she asks. "How can I put my stories before my son? Before The StarQuest? What kind of mother am I?"

"Your stories," the disembodied voice of the dragon Kumba booms into the blackness of the lightless cave, "are your legacy…to your son, to your companions…to your people…to your land. Your stories are your hands and feet…your bones and skin…your heart and lungs. Your stories are the blood and air that course through you, giving you life. Your stories are life. Your life."

I lift my fingers from the keyboard. Of all the vision statements I have crafted for myself over the years, this one may be the most compelling.

"Without your stories," the Great Dragon of Creation continues, "you are barely alive."

Kumba is right. Before *The MoonQuest*, the first of my stories after so many years of running from my creative voice, I was barely alive.

I return my fingers to the keyboard and continue typing. Eight weeks later, a few days shy of the eleventh anniversary of the start of that first aborted first draft, I type the final words of a completed first draft.

I did it.

The Way of the Fool

The Fool lives in the world but not of it, taking no notice of the transient chatterings wafting around her. Instead, he tunes his eyes and ears inward. Her in-sight derives solely from the visions of her essential beingness. The drumbeat of his heart is the only voice he listens for, listens to and heeds.

In a world abundant with opinion-makers, influencers and celebrity endorsements, at a time when there is no lack of competing cries that proclaim the one right way, the Fool makes her own way. It is the way of her inner vision, inner knowingness and inner wisdom, the way that defies comparison, the way that is hers alone to travel. It is the way of her soul's journey. It is the Way of the Fool.

Your Story

Exploration • Awakening Your Vision

Do you know who you are as a creative artist? Do you have a vision for your work? Do you have a vision for the project you're working on? For the project you have barely begun to conceive?

Connecting with and holding a vision for yourself and for your work as a creative artist will help you more easily hold the energy of your creation through the entire process of conception, creation, refinement and release into the world.

One way to hold that vision is by creating a vision statement. What's that? It's a sort of mission statement that expresses your reasons for wanting to put your heart and energy into a particular project or piece of work, that puts your passion into words. A vision statement can be as short as a sentence or as long as a page. It can speak in general terms about your role as a creator or in specific terms about a given creative project — whether you already know what it is or merely that you feel called to create…something.

Nor are vision statements fixed for all time. As your project progresses and you mature through its creation, you may feel called to revisit and revise your vision statement to match your new insights and awareness.

What's your vision for yourself? For your creative work? On the next pages, you will find three ways to help you connect with your vision and craft a vision statement.

What follows first, though, are several of the vision statements I have created over the years.

My Vision Statements

The Way of the Creative Fool

Like so many of my books, *The Way of the Creative Fool* is, ultimately, about intuition, trust and inner knowingness.

Calling on the timeless wisdom of the archetypal Fool, it opens readers' hearts and minds to the creations that already exist, whole and complete, within them.

The book's unique blend of practical tips, dynamic exercises, motivational essays, inspiring meditations and uplifting stories, mine and others', delivers the tools and resources to help creative artists free their creations into the world, with ease — whatever their creative form, medium or genre and whether they are just starting or have been practicing their artistry forever.

My Photography

Photography has been one of my passions since childhood. In fact, I was taking pictures with my Kodak Instamatic, and my Brownie before that, long before my Muse wore down my resistance to becoming a writer.

From the first, even when I wasn't consciously aware of doing it, photography has allowed me to capture my experience of the world around me and, unlike writing, to do it in an instant. It's another way, complementary to writing, of interpreting that world and of sharing my vision of it with others.

The Writer & Storyteller I Am

I didn't plan to write this next one; it emerged spontaneously as I was responding to a Facebook comment. Yet it distills perfectly my passion, purpose and vision as a writer.

Perhaps the sentences I write are the seams that hold me together. Perhaps, that's the real reason I write. Perhaps, ultimately, it's the only reason.

I rediscovered this next one while working on "The Way of the Abundant Fool." As I was searching my computer for a story I hoped to repurpose for one of the steps, I stumbled on a long-forgotten unfinished memoir whose title is itself a sort of vision statement: "All That Matters Is That I'm Writing." Buried in my notes for the project was a draft of the following, crafted from a version of the "Awakening and Embracing Your Vision" meditation scripted later in this section.

I'm a storyteller because I have a gift for painting worlds, galaxies and universes in words and images that bring those realms to life, in words and images that touch and transform others.

I'm a storyteller because it's when I render my emotions and experiences as story that I feel most aligned with my soul's purpose.

I'm a storyteller because that's what I was born to be.

Now it's time for you to craft yours. If you have already written a vision statement, let the following exercises carry you deeper, to a fresh perspective and to any newly awakened aspects of your vision that the experiences kindle.

Your Vision Statement • I

Writing a vision statement can be as simple as getting

into a meditative space and writing on the Muse Stream from the phrase, "My vision for <*title/name/description of project*> is…" or "My work's vision for me is…"

Or allow your work to speak about itself, writing on the Muse Stream from a phrase like, "I am <*title/name/description of project*>. My purpose in your life and in the world is…"

Your Vision Statement • II

Alternatively, ask yourself these questions, but don't use your analytical mind to figure out the answers. Instead, use your visionary mind to sense the answers, to feel the answers, to intuit the answers.

- What is my vision for my project?
- What is my vision for my creative expression?
- What is my vision for myself as a creator? For myself as a creative artist?
- What is my work's vision for me?

Write whatever comes to you, on the Muse Stream. Let it be as long or short as it needs to be. Don't judge or analyze it. It doesn't have to make sense. Let it be what it is.

If no answers come right away, don't think or worry about it. Let the questions swirl around inside you as though you are sipping a vintage wine. Let them steep within you as though you are brewing a fine tea. Meditate, go for a walk or do something else unrelated to your project or creative work. The answers will come when they are ready. The answers will come when you are ready.

Meditation: Awakening and Embracing Your Vision

Have your Way of the Fool journal handy to record your thoughts, feelings and impressions. Allow at least 45 minutes for this experience, including writing time.

A version of this guided meditation is included as part of my downloadable course, "The Heartful Art of Revision: An Intuitive Guide to Editing"[1].

Revisit "Getting Started" for tips on how best to use this book's meditations, visualizations and meditative journeys.

Close your eyes and relax. Let yourself sink into whatever you're sitting on or lying on and take a deep breath, breathing in to your connection with your Muse or whatever you choose to call your creative spirit.

Breathe out your immediate surroundings and all distractions they could inject into your space.

Again, breathe in to your creative source, and feel yourself fill with that energy, that spirit, that openness. And as you breathe out, breathe out all fear and all anxiety.

Let your in-breath carry you deep into your heart, the source of all your creative expression. And as you breathe out, breathe out all worries, all stress, all strain.

If you have a project you're working on, let your breath carry you into a place of profound connection with it, a place of union with it, a place where you and it are one.

Alternatively, let your breath carry you into a place of profound connection with your creatorship, a place of union with it, a place where you and it are one.

As you breathe out, let go all preconceptions, all expectations, all shoulds and musts about your creative project or about your creator self.

---

[1] www.markdavidgerson.com/courses

Allow yourself to surrender to what your creative project is, not what you think it ought to be. Allow yourself to surrender to the creator you are in your deepest core, not the creator you think you are or should be.

Surrender to that. Breathe into that. Be one with that. Whether this experience is connecting you with an individual project or with the core of your creative self, let your next breath open your heart and mind to its vision for itself…to its vision for you.

This experience is not about crafting a vision statement from your conscious mind. It's about letting your work and your deepest creative self speak to you through your heart…through your unconscious mind.

So let your breath carry you there. This breath…and now this breath…and now this breath.

In a moment, I am going to ask you to open your eyes and write on the Muse Stream from a phrase I will give you. This phrase will be an expression of your vision for your work or of your vision for yourself.

Again, not a conscious expression. A deeper, truer, fuller expression. Don't be attached to the phrase. If some other way of expressing your vision comes to you, go with that.

Regardless, go wherever the Muse Stream takes you… even if it appears to be taking you off course…even if it makes no logical sense.

Don't judge what comes. Don't actively choose what to write or where to go with it. Let it carry you where you need to go. Creating on the Muse Stream is always about letting and allowing. Creating on the Muse Stream is always about surrender.

Allow to come whatever comes. Length doesn't matter. Form and language don't matter. Your conscious mind's understanding of what you have written doesn't matter.

What matters is that, at some level, you and your

creation sing the same song and that that harmony supports you as you refine and enrich your creatorship.

So once again be conscious of your breath…of your physical body, of the physical space you now occupy, as you allow your breath to return you to full awareness.

And when you feel ready, taking all the time you need, gently open your eyes and be fully present, ready to write on the Muse Stream from this phrase: My vision for <*"my creative project" or "myself as the creator/creative artist I am"*> is…

If you know your project's title or working title, include it. If you don't, include its form — for example, "my painting" or "my garden" or "my book." If you're not yet clear on its form, use the phrase "my creative project."

My vision for <*"my creative project" or "myself as the creator/creative artist I am"*> is…

Follow the words where they take you, and let your pen pull your hand across the page or dance across your keyboard as you surrender to the journey…as you surrender to your vision.

Creating on the Muse Stream

Revisit "Creating on the Muse Stream" from Step #1, and repeat the exercise.

When You're Finished…

Now that you have more clarity about your creative vision, how was this creative session different from others you have experienced? In process? In content? In emotional response? In resistance? Take a few minutes and note those differences, along with how the experience made you feel, in your Way of the Fool journal.

The Way of the Visionary Fool

Hildegard von Bingen was three when she had the first of what she would later come to describe as "this vision in my soul." Even after she was given over to a Benedictine monastery at age eight, she kept those visions largely to herself.

When at forty-two she felt called by God "to write down that which you see and hear," she hesitated. Who was she, she asked herself, to record these "reflections of the living light," as she called them.

Did her hesitation cause the serious illnesses that followed? Hildegard came to believe that it did. Once she surrendered to the divine call, she launched into one of the most astounding outpourings of visionary creativity in history: luminous art, groundbreaking musical compositions, and writings on botany, mystical theology and natural healing that were centuries ahead of her time. She even invented a language.

Today, nearly nine hundred years after her death, Hildegard von Bingen remains a powerful role model for anyone called to express a creative vision in the world. "Dare to declare who you are," she is known to have said, a message as relevant today as it was in medieval times.

Hildegard von Bingen was canonized in 2012, something of a formality, as she had already been venerated as a saint for centuries. Not surprisingly, St. Hildegard is a patron saint of writers and musicians.

My Story: Coda

I was seven months from starting my first first draft of *The StarQuest* when, one fall morning, I found myself ambling along Sedona's Airport Loop trail. Back then, that was one of my favorite morning hikes, not least because of the breathtaking vista that opens up a few minutes from the trailhead. As the path curves southward to hug the mesa's scrubby slope, you're suddenly confronted with an unimpeded view of three red-rock formations: Bell Rock, Cathedral Rock and Courthouse Butte.

Bell and Cathedral are the better known of the three, but it was to Courthouse that my eyes were drawn that morning, probably because it always reminded me of the pink-stoned Castle Rose, a key location in *The MoonQuest*. As I often did on these walks, I stopped and gazed toward it, feeling within its majesty the power of my still-unpublished story. This time, though, I felt something more. Or, rather, I heard something, as clearly as if someone were standing next to me: "Your books will support you."

A dozen years later, *The StarQuest* did just that. Not directly, of course, because the book wasn't finished, let alone published. Yet as I honored my commitment to, finally, completing a first draft, and through whatever Muse-inspired alchemy was at play, money began showing up, mostly from a sudden influx of coaching clients.

Within a few months, I walked out of that Hobby Lobby stockroom for the last time. Soon after, thanks to all my newly freed-up time and energy, I dropped the final period on a first draft of *The StarQuest*.

By then, *The MoonQuest* had already been published. Three years and five drafts later, *The StarQuest* joined it on bookstore shelves.

Declaration

I, *your name*, awaken, acknowledge, access, and express the full depth and richness of my creative vision — for myself and for my work. As the Creative Fool that I am, I know I am always supported by that vision, always and in all ways that matter. And so it is.

Beyond the 12½th Step

Let dreams fuel your sight.
The Bard of Bryn Doon,
The Legend of Q'ntana, Book 4

I Believe in You

It's easy, as a creative artist, to feel discouraged and disheartened, to feel defeated and destroyed. It's easy to shout "I'm done" and give up.

Don't do it.

Whatever its source, don't yield to the despair. Whatever has sparked it, don't give in to the hopelessness. Whatever has triggered it, don't give in to the desperation and depression.

Feel what you feel, always. But don't let yourself stop there. Don't let yourself get stuck there. Don't let yourself be paralyzed into inaction.

Whoever you are, whatever your story, you have done so much, come so far. It may not always feel that way, but it's true.

Don't squander all you have accomplished and achieved by stopping now. Don't give up on your dreams. Don't give up on your passion. Don't give up on your creativity…on your creations. Don't give up on yourself.

I believe in you.

Meditation: Believe in You

Have your Way of the Fool journal handy to record your thoughts, feelings and impressions. Allow 5 minutes for this meditative/journaling experience.

"Believe in You" is adapted from "You Are a Writer," which is recorded on my album "The Voice of the Muse Companion: Guided Meditations for Writers" and is available for download or streaming.[1]

Revisit "Getting Started" to find out how to access the recording, as well as for tips on how best to use all this book's meditations, visualizations and meditative journeys.

Close your eyes and take a few deep breaths, in and out. In and out. In and out.

Allow your breath to relax you, to center you, to carry you to an oasis of peace deep within you.

Breathe in to that oasis. Breathe in to that stillness. Breathe in to that calm.

And as you breathe out, let all the stresses and strains of your day, of your week, of your life melt away.

Let all the struggles melt away.

Let all the worry and anxiety melt away.

Let each fresh inhalation carry you deeper into the heart of who you are…into the heart of all you are…into the heart of the creator you are. Into the truth of who you are…into the truth of the creator you are.

And let each exhalation release all the not-enoughs and not-good-enoughs. All the shoulds, musts and supposed-tos. All the can'ts, can't dos and can't be's. All the places within you where you do not believe in yourself or cannot believe in yourself.

Now, breathe in. Breathe in to the light you are. Breathe in to the divinity you are. Breathe in to the wisdom you

---

[1] Search the relevant site/store for "Mark David Gerson you are a writer."

are. Breathe in to the infinite potential you are. Breathe in to the infinite creative potential you are.

Breathe into the Creative Fool that you are. Breathe out comparisons. What others are or have done does not matter. What others have created or accomplished does not matter. What others think of what you have created or have accomplished does not matter. What others say about what you have created or have accomplished does not matter.

All that matters is this moment. All that matters is the divine perfection of this moment. All that matters is your divine perfection in this moment.

So breathe in to that.

Fully.

Deeply.

Completely.

You are a powerful creator…a creative artist of passion, strength and, yes, courage. For every creative act is an act of courage.

Acknowledge that courage. Breathe into that courage. Breathe into it deeply. Breathe into it with every ounce of your innate creative gifts…of your life force. Breathe into your knowingness of that. Breathe into your certainty of that. Breathe into it and believe it. Breathe into it and believe in you.

Let me say it again.

You are a powerful creator…a creative artist of passion, strength and courage. I believe that.

I believe in you.

Now, speak it, silently within yourself.

> *I am a powerful creator…a creative artist of passion, strength and courage. I believe in me.*

Again…

> *I am a powerful creator…a creative artist of passion, strength and courage. I believe in me.*

One more time…

> *I am a powerful creator…a creative artist of passion, strength and courage. I believe in me.*

Now say it out loud.

Do more than speak the words. Infuse those words with the full power of your conviction and the full conviction of your power. Infuse them with all your belief and all your knowingness. Infuse them with all the emotion that underlies all that.

> *I am a powerful creator…a creative artist of passion, strength and courage. I believe in me.*

And again…

> *I am a powerful creator…a creative artist of passion, strength and courage. I believe in me.*

One more time…

> *I am a powerful creator…a creative artist of passion, strength and courage. I believe in me.*

Let these words stay with you, and continue to speak them as often as you can, as often as you dare, knowing them to be true, feeling the truth in them. Speak them again and again and again, for they are true.

One More Time…

From that place of certainty in your artistry and the gift of your creativity, revisit "Creating on the Muse Stream" from Step #1, and repeat the exercise.

When You're Finished...

Now that you have affirmed your absolute belief in yourself and in your creativity, how was this creative session different from others you have experienced? In process? In content? In emotional response? In resistance? Take a few minutes and note those differences, along with how the experience made you feel, in your Way of the Fool journal.

Say Yes to You!

In my novel *Sara's Year*, two of the main characters enter their teen years with powerful dreams and ambitions.

One yearns to be a writer; the other, an artist.

By the time they reach their early twenties, however, both dreams have been abandoned. Life has a way of getting in the way when we let it...and both those women did.

The good news for one of the two is that, ultimately, she not only revives a dream she believed to have been lost for good, she finds a way to dive into it and live it...with monumental success.

It wasn't too late for Sara to follow her dreams and it's never too late for you to follow yours...even the ones you thought you had given up. It's never too late to rekindle the hope that has shriveled into hopelessness. And it's never too early to give up on the idea of giving up.

What's your dream for your creativity? Know that whatever it is, however improbable you might judge it to be, it is no more impossible for you than it was for Sara.

Nearly every success story begins with an "impossible" dream. Nearly every "overnight success" was years in the making.

What about your dreams? Have you abandoned them? Stuffed them in the back of a drawer because they seemed so unreachable?

Open that drawer. Reach your hand in. Gently. Touch it. Reconnect with it. Reconnect with yourself.

Have you committed to your passion…to your creativity…to your dreams? Are you acting on that commitment?

If not, *now* is the time. It doesn't matter whether you can set aside five minutes a day or five hours. It doesn't matter whether you know in this moment what your creative journey is about or where it will take you.

Every journey begins with a single step. Every creative project begins with a moment of choice.

Make that choice. Now.

Open your heart again. Open your heart to the vision. Open your heart to yourself. Open your heart to your life. Say yes to you. Say yes to the creator you are!

A Community of Creative Fools

Too often, we don't recognize our creativity, can't see our talent, refuse to acknowledge our gifts. That's not surprising, given how solitary and insular many creative endeavors can be, given how untrained so many people are in the words and actions that support another's creativity.

Groups can be a powerful antidote to that. When we surround ourselves with like-minded, like-spirited creatives, we can't help but move forward, whatever the specifics of our goals.

That's because outlooks and attitudes are contagious. It's too easy to fall back into negativity and pessimism when those around us come from those perspectives. It's too easy to doubt our dreams when those around us tear them down instead of encouraging them.

If we can't always choose our family and work colleagues, we can always choose our friends and creative colleagues. Start spending time with fellow creators who are focused on their dreams, who embrace possibility, not improbability, whose ways of thinking and ways of being reinforce your goals, people who celebrate you and your creativity.

One way to do this is to form a Community of Creative Fools. By coming together with others on a similar journey, you will have an opportunity to take all you have experienced and read in these pages and multiply it manyfold through the empowering support of others.

It's easy: Share *The Way of the Creative Fool*, your enthusiasm and your commitment with a few like-spirited artists — in your field or in a mix of fields — and, voilà, you are part of a powerful vortex of motivation and inspiration.

These days, you and your fellow Creative Fools need not be in the same city or the same part of the world. Social networks make it easy to find others who share your passion and outlook. And videoconferencing platforms make time-zone conflicts the only barrier to meaningful connection across the miles.

However you format your Community of Creative Fools, consider these suggestions…

Check-In

When working on a creative project, mutual accountability can be a powerful motivator. Set aside time at every get-together for all members to share their experiences. Keep contributions brief. This is not a time for mutual therapy, nor is it a time to make others feel guilty if they have done little since your last meeting. It's a time for accountability, kudos and support. You want to make sure time remains available for…

Creating/Sharing

Some groups use these meetups as an opportunity to create together. Of course, this isn't always practical. If it is, set aside sufficient time for it.

Alternatively, pick or adapt an exercise or meditation from this book or create your own. If it's a meditation, designate one member to lead it, and be sure to rotate that role from one get-together to the next.

Afterward, allow whoever wants to share what they have experienced that opportunity. Remember: This is a community of support, not a critiquing group, so revisit the Explorations in Step #11, paying extra attention to my "Seven Be's of Empowered Feedback."

Rotation

Avoid leader burnout by taking turns communicating with members, moderating/hosting and choosing the activities/exercises.

Frequency

Agree to meet regularly, at least monthly.

Numbers

Keep the size of your group small enough that everyone who wants to has an opportunity to share their work, their goals, their dreams and their experiences — if not at every meeting, then at every second or third.

Other Ideas

Meeting in person? Create a space and ambiance conducive to creativity, community and focus, one that's quiet and where you and your fellow creatives won't be disturbed. Make sure, for example, that all cellphones are switched off. Consider playing meditative music as people arrive to set the atmosphere. People bond well over food, and many groups incorporate regular or occasional potlucks into their get-togethers.

Meeting online? Make sure all members join your virtual community from somewhere quiet where they won't be interrupted or disturbed. Encourage them to stay focused on the get-together by quitting all unnecessary applications and by muting all sounds unrelated to the group experience.

Remember, this is a community of Fools. Don't take yourselves or each other too seriously. Give yourselves permission to be Fool-ish (and foolish)…and have fun!

The Way of the Creative Fool and You

WHAT'S YOUR STORY? I'd love to hear about your experiences with *The Way of the Creative Fool* and about any of the ways you have freed up or expanded your creative expression through working with this book's Fool-ish principles.

To that end, I have created a dedicated page on my website — www.markdavidgerson.com/yourstories — and I invite you to share your stories and comments there.

What you post will remain private and anonymous unless you give me explicit permission to use it, with or without your name.

Share your thoughts and feelings, your stumbles and successes, and your stories. Let yourself be vulnerable. And if you have questions, feel free to ask them.

While I can't promise to respond to every submission, I will read them all and get back to you wherever possible. I look forward with great anticipation to hearing from you.

Afterword: The Creative Fool and I

WHEN I WAS, FINALLY, approaching the end of a first draft of *The StarQuest* (see "My Story," Step #12½), I had a fairly clear idea of how, in the closing scenes, one of my antagonists would meet her downfall. At least, I thought I did.

Then, on my final day's work on that initial draft, as I was letting the penultimate scene write itself, this character did something unanticipated. Something extraordinary. Something so incredible that it was beyond anything my logical mind could have conjured up.

More than that, it underscored what I had begun to recognize as one of the book's central themes, and it did it in a way that was mindblowingly original. (It was *my* mind that was blown!)

But that isn't the best part of the story.

As thrilled as I was by this inspired ending, I worried that I would have to make radical changes to my next *StarQuest* draft for that ending to make sense. Yet when I read the draft all the way through, I was stunned to discover that *no* such changes were needed.

I said in Step #7 that the Muse is smarter than we are. If I needed proof of that, my first draft of *The StarQuest* provided it. By listening for the story, listening to the story, and getting out of my way and trusting the story, I had written to that ending without realizing it.

My Muse was smarter than I was. So was my story…my creation.

Whatever you are creating, that creation knows itself better than you do…than you ever will. Of course, it does. It's a sentient entity with a life force and wisdom of its own, with a will and imperative of its own. If you trust it to exercise that will and imperative through you, your experience as its creator will astonish you with its ease and free-flow.

Some years back, a visual artist came to me for coaching help. She sensed a new style birthing through her but didn't know how to access it. All she could do was stare at her blank canvas in mounting frustration.

"Your only job is to hold the brush," I counseled her, "because that's the one thing your painting can never do by itself. If you get out of the way and trust the brush to move your hand across the canvas, your painting will reveal itself to you."

She did, and it did.

Trust. That's the point of the Muse Stream: to help you to trust your Muse, your creative source, your unconscious mind, your intuitive self, your higher self, God, Spirit…whatever you choose to call the infinite indwelling presence that is at the same time your wisest, most creative aspect and the ineffable universality that is the sum of all that is. Put another way, the Muse Stream is about trusting that if you move from the driver's seat of your creative journey to its passenger seat, you will free into the world work that is more engaging, compelling and inspired than anything you could have planned, plotted, outlined, sketched out or consciously crafted.

That has certainly been my experience, and not exclusively with *The StarQuest*. Whenever I let my Muse take the wheel — whatever I'm working on, and whatever its form, medium or genre — I'm always transported to new, uncharted worlds. The ride can feel manic and out of control. It can feel crazy, terrifyingly crazy. But it's also exhilarating, and it never fails to take me where I need to go. The best part? In freeing my creations to live their full potential, they always free me to live mine.

That's the Way of the Creative Fool.

Mark David Gerson
Scottsdale, AZ
December 2025

Appreciation

BACK IN STEP #2, I shared about the Toronto writing workshop that radically altered the trajectory of my creative life. More than thirty years later, I still owe a debt of gratitude to Caren Pummell, the colleague who badgered me into signing up for it, and Carole H. Leckner, who taught it. Without Caren's uncharacteristic persistence and Carole's extraordinary mentorship, there could be no *Way of the Creative Fool*. That's because there would have been no creative trajectory. No books. No art. No music. No teaching, coaching or mentoring. No authentic creative expression. It all began with that water cooler conversation and kicked off with Carole's workshop.

Reaching farther back into the past, I can't not acknowledge my mother. Although absent now for nearly forty years, her infectious love of reading planted seeds in me that, with Carole Leckner's guidance and support, blossomed into my unquenchable love of writing and storytelling and, ultimately, into this book.

Thanks, too, to all the supremely creative women and men I have been privileged to teach, coach and mentor through this past year and over the decades: Your passion, strength, courage and commitment never fail to inspire me to go deeper, to speak truer and to create more fearlessly. This book could not have happened without you.

If writing a book is, more often than not, a solo pursuit, it helps to have a team of cheerleaders rooting for you from the sidelines, if only to remind you that you *can* do it when you think you can't, and that you're not crazy when you're certain you are. Through my journey with *The Way of the Creative Fool*, I must single out Sander Dov Freedman, who has been cheering me on for longer than anyone I know; Aalia Kazan, who has never stopped believing in me and my work; Rebecca Michaels, who is always ready with long-distance support and encouragement; and my daughter, Guinevere, among the greatest gifts in my life and always an inspiration.

In this book's Afterword, I talk about how each of our creations is a sentient entity with its own wisdom, will and imperative. That creative intelligence manifests itself in my life in myriad ways, particularly with my books, each of which knows where it wants to be written and has no hesitation about rearranging my life to make that possible.

With some books, like *The MoonQuest*, that has necessitated multiple moves across international boundaries as well as state lines. *The Way of the Creative Fool* has been more single-minded, dropping me in Scottsdale, Arizona and leaving me here for the duration. Metro Phoenix is not a place I ever expected to call home, or thought I would want to call home. But as with all my books and creative projects, *The Way of the Creative Fool* is smarter than I am, and I'm grateful to be here.

I'm also grateful to the staff of Sonesta Simply Suites Phoenix Scottsdale, my temporary home while I worked on the book, and to the baristas of the Starbucks in Kierland Commons, where I wrote pretty much all of it. By now, many of the baristas there know my name and my unusual go-to drink, which some start ringing up before I get to the register.

Pull the Fool card from any tarot deck card and, however the figure is represented, you will nearly always see it accompanied by a dog. Mine is Kyri, the chihuahua-terrier mix who came into my life while I was writing *The Way the Imperfect Fool*. My constant companion since then (including at the Kierland Starbucks, where he is considerably more popular with its staff and customers than I can ever hope to be), Kyri has kept me sane, or at least as sane as it's possible for any creative artist to be. Moreover, he never stops reminding me that being creative means not taking life too seriously. He has saved my life more than once, and I'm profoundly grateful to him.

As with *The MoonQuest* and *Sara's Year*, each of which I viewed as a one-off and each of which quickly turned itself into the first in a series, a cycle of *Way of the Fool* books was never in my plans. Yet here we are. So to the readers and fans of my three previous *Fool* books, thank you. Without your testimonials and enthusiasm, I would have been unlikely to write a fourth.

Finally, to my Muse: Thank you for your gentle and not-so-gentle nudges. My life would be infinitely poorer without the well of creative ideas you send my way.

About the Author

MARK DAVID GERSON is a photographer, visionary artist and screenwriter, and the award-winning author of more than two dozen books. His nonfiction includes popular titles for writers and other creatives, inspiring personal growth books and compelling memoirs. As a novelist, he is best known for *The Legend of Q'ntana* fantasy series and for *The Sara Stories*, set largely in his hometown of Montreal.

Please visit Mark David's website, www.markdavidgerson.com, and follow him on social media.

Reviews help! Please consider posting a review to your favorite book sites.

Be Inspired by More of Mark David's Folly!

Get Your Copies Today!